Different Seas

I Talk You Talk Press

Copyright © 2018 I Talk You Talk Press

ISBN: 978-4-907056-76-6

www.italkyoutalk.com

info@italkyoutalk.com

All rights reserved. No part of this publication may be resold, reproduced, stored in retrieval system, copied in any form or by any means, electronic, mechanical, photocopying, recording or otherwise transmitted without the prior written permission from the publisher. You must not circulate this publication in any format, online or otherwise.

This is a work of fiction. Names, characters, businesses, organizations, products, places, events and incidents are either the products of the author's imagination or are used in a fictitious manner. We have no affiliation with any existing companies mentioned in this story. Any resemblance to actual persons, living or dead, existing stories or actual events is purely coincidental.

Although the author and publisher have made every effort to ensure that the contents of this book were correct at press time, the author and publisher do not assume and hereby disclaim any liability to any party for any loss, damage, or disruption caused by errors or omissions, whether such errors or omissions result from negligence, accident, or any other cause.

For more information, see the Copyright Notice on our website.

Image copyright: Scenery: © Y. Papadimitriou - Fotolia.com #103361027 Standard License
People: © Kirsty Pargeter - Fotolia.com#41652896 Standard License

CONTENTS

A DANGEROUS CELEBRATION

1. No worries	1
2. Planning a party	3
3. A surprise for Shelley	6
4. Barbara and Shelley's house	9
5. Paddington	13
6. Brisbane	17
7. Party time!	19
8. Invasion	22
9. The plan	27
10. The police	32
11. Time to leave	35

DEATH ON AN ISLAND

1. Dimitris is interested	37
2. Shall we telephone?	41
3. Surprise visitors	46
4. Sofia's story	50
5. Plans	55
6. To Santorini	58
7. The house of horror	61
8. Nothing left	65
9. It's only Thursday	68
10. A holiday in Greece	72
Thank You	74
About the Author	76

A DANGEROUS CELEBRATION

1. NO WORRIES

This is heaven, thought Chrysa. She was lying on a sun lounge under a huge old eucalyptus tree. The sun was hot, but there was a soft breeze. Chrysa could smell the sea air.

I feel so relaxed and happy. I could stay here forever.

She turned her head and looked at Akina. Akina was lying on a sun lounge next to her. Akina had a big sunhat over her face. She was asleep.

"Get it! Get it!" It was Jarmo's voice. Chrysa sat up, and looked across the grass to the beach. Jarmo and Shelley were playing beach volleyball with Pachai and Hehu.

She watched the game for a while. Blond Jarmo and red-haired Shelley were much shorter than Pachai and Hehu, but it seemed Jarmo and Shelley were winning.

It's nice to have this time at the beach, thought Chrysa. *We did so much during our first week in Sydney. I loved the bike tours around the harbour, the museums and the great restaurants and bars. And that crazy rugby league match we went to. I didn't understand the rules, but it was very exciting. This is quiet, but it's fun too. I love it here in Australia. There is no pressure. No stress. Everyone is so relaxed.*

Chrysa laughed quietly. *Everyone says 'no worries'. I asked the baggage handler in the airport to lift my bag off the carousel. He smiled at me and said 'no worries'. When I asked the woman on the front desk of the hotel in Sydney about the weather, she said 'No worries. It won't rain today'. That's why I feel good — no one has any worries. Everything is OK.*

The volleyball match was finished. Shelley was pulling a T-shirt on over her bikini. Jarmo and Pachai were taking down the net. Soon the four friends were walking up from the beach towards the grass in the front of the house.

"Was it a good game?" asked Chrysa.

"Very good," said Shelley, laughing. "Jarmo and I won!"

"I'm thirsty," said Pachai. "Does anyone else want a drink?"

"Yes, please," said Shelley. "Coke would be nice."

"Coke for me too, please," said Jarmo.

Jarmo and Shelley sat down on the grass next to Chrysa's chair.

"I'll help you," said Hehu to Pachai. "Chrysa? Do you want anything?"

"Some iced water, please," answered Chrysa.

Pachai and Hehu went up the steps and into the house.

"This is a magical place," said Jarmo. "We're lucky to stay here. Your mother has very kind friends, Shelley."

Shelley smiled. "Well, I don't know this friend very well. I only met him once. But I guess he is very rich. Big houses like this one in Hawks Nest cost a million dollars, or maybe more."

"Is he your mother's boyfriend?" asked Jarmo.

"I think so. I hope so. My father died almost twenty years ago. My mother must be lonely sometimes."

Pachai and Hehu came onto the grass with two trays of drinks and some snacks.

Jarmo stood up and went to Akina's sun lounge. He lifted the sunhat off her face.

"Wake up!" he said. "Time for a drink and a snack." He took his coke from Pachai and dropped an ice cube on Akina's neck.

"Waaa!" shouted Akina. She sat up and punched Jarmo.

"Ow!" said Jarmo holding his arm. "That hurt!"

Everyone laughed.

"Be careful, Jarmo," smiled Pachai. "Akina is a tiny person, but she can punch very hard. It's dangerous to tease her."

Hehu passed a glass of iced water to Chrysa.

"Thank you." Chrysa smiled at Hehu.

"No worries," answered Hehu.

2. PLANNING A PARTY

More than 200km away in Darling Point, Sydney, a man and a woman were sitting in the living room of a large modern house. The huge windows were open, and the sun shone through onto the white furniture and the dramatic modern art on the walls.

The woman was casually dressed in a white T-shirt and shorts. She was quite small, and had red hair. She looked about fifty years old. Her name was Barbara Rakena.

The man was older. He had white hair, and was very tanned. He took an open bottle of champagne from the table between them. He poured two glasses and handed one to the woman.

"Are you sure?" he asked. "Are you sure you want to marry me?"

Barbara laughed. "Of course I am sure I want to marry you. Why do you ask?"

"I was thinking about your daughter. I have only met her once. She looks a lot like you. She is an only child. Since your husband died, you have been a family of two. I'm worried she will not want you to marry me."

"Why not? Shelley has a good job here in Sydney. She has many friends. Her school friends and her work friends. And the group that came to Australia last week. Shelley is very close to them too."

"You told me about them. It's unusual isn't it? They are six young people from different countries, and with different lifestyles. And they meet twice a year for a vacation. How did it happen?"

"Well, Hehu is Shelley's cousin. She has known him all her life. He is a farmer from the north of New Zealand. When Shelley was working in London, Hehu went to visit her. They booked a cycling trip in France, but it was cancelled. The others, the young man from Finland, the Indian man who lives in Paris, and the two young women from Japan and Greece planned to take the same tour. Somehow they got together, and rented a holiday house on the coast of Brittany. That's how it started. Then they saved the life of an old Frenchman. When he died, he left money to the six of them in his will. They use it to get together when they can.

"It was nice of you to lend them your beach house in Hawks Nest. Shelley called me yesterday. She said they were having a wonderful time."

The man laughed. "I wasn't nice. I wanted to make sure we would be alone this weekend, so I could propose to you. I want to make a toast."

The man refilled his champagne glass and held it up towards Barbara.

"To Barbara, the future Mrs Bill Curtis."

He drank the champagne. He leant across the table and kissed Barbara.

"I am so happy," he said. "I want everyone to know we are engaged, and plan to marry. Shall we have a big party?"

"I guess so," smiled Barbara. "Will we have it here?"

"We could have the party here, but I was thinking about my yacht. We could have a party on my yacht."

"Your yacht! You have a yacht?" Barbara was very surprised.

"Yes, I have a yacht," answered Bill. "I guess I forgot to tell you."

"And it's big enough to have a party on?" Barbara was still surprised.

"Yes. We could invite maybe thirty or forty people. It is big enough."

Barbara was quiet. She looked down at her hands. Her engagement ring with its pink diamonds sparkled in the sun. She looked around the large room with its expensive furniture and artwork. She looked at the black marble side table, and the vase of white orchids.

"Are you OK?" Bill was worried.

Barbara looked at him. "Yes. I'm fine," she said. "But I am not used to so much money. After my husband died, I worked hard. I always had enough money for Shelley and me, but we didn't have a lot. I wish you were not so rich."

Bill laughed. "I will give all my money away if it will make you happy. But Barbara, I worked very hard for my money. I spent my life in the desert. That's why I am sixty years old, and I have never had a wife. I have no children. And I don't keep all my money."

Barbara nodded. She knew that Bill was very generous to many charities. He gave a lot of money away.

"I'm sorry, Bill," she said. "I am being silly. I want to marry you. I want to live in this house with you. And of course, we will have our engagement party on your yacht."

3. A SURPRISE FOR SHELLEY

That evening, Akina and Pachai cooked dinner on the barbeque at the house at Hawks Nest. They grilled prawns and tofu. Akina cooked noodles and vegetables on the barbeque plate. "It's called yaki-soba," she told Pachai.

Pachai tasted some. "It's very tasty," he said.

"Usually I add some pork," Akina said. "But you and Shelley don't eat meat. It is still good without meat."

When the food was cooked, they took it to the table on the terrace in front of the house. Jarmo and Hehu were sitting at the table drinking beer. Chrysa and Shelley were in the kitchen.

"Time to eat!" called Pachai. Shelley came out to the terrace carrying a large tray of fruit. Chrysa followed with water, wine and glasses.

The food was great. After they finished eating, they stayed outside, drinking the last of the wine, and eating strawberries and slices of melon. The air was still warm. It was a beautiful night.

"This is wonderful," said Jarmo. "But we take the train back to Sydney tomorrow. Then we have six more days. You told us you had a surprise for us, Shelley. What is it? What is the plan for the rest of our vacation?"

"I hope you are going to like it," said Shelley. "So far you have seen big buildings in Sydney. You have seen beaches and harbours, but Australia has more than that. Australia has hills and lakes and forests and deserts. I want you to see as much as possible. My mother's cousin has a big sheep farm. He has accommodation for the shearers. The shearing finished months ago and the accommodation is empty, so we can stay there."

"Shearers?" asked Akina. "What are shearers?"

"Shearers travel around farms to cut the wool off the sheep," said Hehu. "Sometimes there are thousands of sheep. The shearers stay on the farm until the job is done, so farmers have to build somewhere for them to stay."

"It is a great idea!" said Jarmo. "When do we go? How will we get there?"

"We will arrive in Sydney about lunchtime tomorrow. We will rent a car. Hehu and I can drive. It will take about four hours to get there. On the way, we will drive through the Blue Mountains National Park. The farm is on the edge of another national park. It is called Wollemi. There is a lake close by as well."

Everyone was very excited.

"Can we ride horses?" asked Pachai. "I have never been on a horse, but I want to learn."

"Of course you can ride," smiled Shelley. "There are many horses on the farm. Hehu can teach you how to ride. I can ride quite well, but Hehu is better than me. His father took him on a horse before he could walk."

As Shelley was talking, her smartphone rang. She looked at it. "Oh, it's my mother. I wonder why she is calling me. Excuse me, I should answer her call."

Shelley took her smartphone inside the house. She was gone for a long time. When she came back, she was carrying another bottle of wine.

She sat down at the table and opened the bottle. She poured a glass and drank it very quickly.

Everyone was very surprised. Shelley never drank a lot of alcohol.

"Is something wrong?" asked Chrysa.

"No. Yes. No," said Shelley.

Hehu got up from his chair and walked around the table. He knelt down and put his arm around Shelley.

"What is it?" he asked.

Shelley shook her head. Then she said, "Change of plan. We can't go to the farm."

"Is your mother's cousin ill?" asked Akina.

"No," answered Shelley. "My mother just got engaged. She is

going to marry Bill Curtis. The man who lent us this house."

"Is that a problem for you?" asked Pachai.

"No. No. I got a shock, but I am very happy for her. She has been alone for too long. The problem is they plan to have a celebration party next Saturday. Today is Tuesday. There is not enough time to go to the farm. I am so sorry."

Everyone said, "Don't worry. It doesn't matter. We will do things in Sydney instead."

"Well, there is one bonus," said Shelley. "The party is on Bill Curtis' yacht, and you are all invited!"

4. BARBARA AND SHELLEY'S HOUSE

Shelley was worried. It was Wednesday morning. They were taking the train back to Sydney, but Shelley didn't know where they could stay. Plans had changed. They were not going to hire a car, and drive north into the New South Wales countryside. The farm holiday was cancelled.

The first week, everyone had stayed in a hotel near Kings Cross. Shelley had made the reservations two months before the others arrived. It was very noisy, but it was clean and cheap, but now it was full. That hotel was full all week. Shelley could not get new reservations. She couldn't find cheap hotel rooms anywhere. She sent a text to her mother.

--- *We can't find a hotel. Could everyone stay at our house?* ---

Shelley's mother answered quickly.

--- *I am going to stay at Bill's house this week. Of course you can all stay in our house.* ---

When they arrived in Sydney they took two more trains and finally arrived in a tree-lined street in Paddington.

"Here it is," said Shelley. She pointed to a narrow two-storey house with a pretty garden and iron railings on the porches and balconies. "It's small, but I think we can all find a place to sleep. At least there are two bathrooms!"

She walked down the narrow path to the front door and unlocked it. They all walked into a long narrow room. It was a kitchen, dining room and living room all in one. It had glass doors that opened to a sunny garden at the back.

"It's lovely!" said Chrysa. "And it's so close to the centre of Sydney!"

"Is it your mother's house?" asked Akina.

"Yes," answered Shelley. "It was her grandfather's house. Of course, it looked very different when he lived here! When he died, he left it to my mother. That was just before my father died. So my mother and I always had somewhere to live. She has altered and renovated it slowly when she had enough money."

"OK. Now you guys stay here. I will show Akina and Chrysa where they can sleep."

Chrysa and Akina followed Shelley up a narrow stairway.

"I will sleep in my mother's room," said Shelley. "And you can sleep in my room." She opened the door to a sunny room decorated in yellow and white.

"My bed is narrow, but we have a camp bed in the attic. If we move the desk, it will fit in. The bathroom is next door."

Downstairs again, Shelley explained to the guys about where they would sleep.

"These sofas in the living room open up to make beds. So they are for Pachai and Jarmo. Hehu, you will have to sleep on the floor. But we do have an air bed."

Hehu smiled. "That's OK. I'm good at sleeping on the floor."

Hehu climbed into the attic and brought down the camp bed and the air bed. Shelley found towels, sheets, pillows and quilts for everyone. Chrysa made tea and coffee. They sat around the dining table and chatted.

"We will have to go out a lot," said Shelley. "The house is too small for six people."

"It will be fine," said Chrysa. "We will be very comfortable. Your mother is so kind to let us stay here."

Chrysa's family was very rich. Chrysa could easily go and stay in an expensive hotel. She could pay for everyone else to stay there too.

Pachai seems to have money too, she thought. *His clothes are expensive, and he wears a beautiful gold watch. He is happy to do everything as cheaply as possible. It is more fun to be the same as everyone else. The money from M. Villemont pays for the airfares, but I am sure Jarmo, Akina, Hehu and Shelley have to save money for our holidays.*

"I must call my mother," said Shelley. "I want to be sure she is happy."

Shelley took out her phone and walked out into the garden.

"When and where are we going to eat? I'm starving," said Jarmo. He took his iPad out of his bag and started looking on the Internet. "Paddington is great!" he said. "There are so many bars and restaurants. Shelley will know the best ones."

"Are there any clothes shops?" asked Chrysa.

"Clothes shops?" Jarmo was surprised. "Why do you want clothes shops?"

Chrysa put her coffee cup on the table and looked around at everyone.

"A party on a yacht. That means we need party clothes."

"No, Chrysa," said Hehu. "People will wear shorts and sandals. Clothes for fishing and drinking beer!"

"I don't think so," answered Chrysa. "Think about it! It's not five or six people sitting on boxes and drinking beer. We have been invited. It must be a big party. I think this will be a party with a band and cocktails and waiters. I think the dress code will be semi-formal. I didn't pack any clothes for parties like that. I must go out and buy a dress."

"Me too!" said Akina. "I only have cotton sun dresses with me. I didn't pack a party dress. We'll ask Shelley where the best shops are."

Shelley came back from the garden. "My mother is busy. She is arranging the party, and she is shopping for clothes."

"What kind of party is it?" asked Hehu. "Is it casual?"

"No," answered Shelley. "I think it will be a fancy party. The yacht is in a marina near Brisbane. At first Bill thought he would tell the crew to bring it down to Sydney. Then he changed his mind. His friends live all over Australia. It doesn't matter to them where the party is. So, on Saturday, we will all fly up to Brisbane. After the party, we will stay in a hotel. On Sunday, we will fly back to Sydney. Bill is paying for everything."

"So we all need clothes," said Chrysa. "Should the guys wear suits?"

"Suits!" Shelley was amazed. "I don't think so. I'll call my mother and ask."

Shelley spoke to her mother again. When she finished the call, she smiled at Hehu, and said, "Lucky escape for you. No suits. Bill hates suits. He doesn't own one. So smart casual for the guys, and pretty dresses for us. But I'm not wearing a dress. I never wear dresses."

"Enough!" shouted Jarmo. "Clothes are boring! Let's go out and party!"

Chrysa laughed. "OK, Jarmo. You're right. Tonight we'll go to a restaurant and then find a nightclub and dance. Tomorrow, we'll go shopping."

5. PADDINGTON

Jarmo was right. Paddington was a great place to have a good night out. They ate in a small Italian café, then went to a nightclub and danced until 2:00am. The next morning, everyone slept late.

Shelley made pancakes for brunch, and they ate on the sunny terrace behind the house. Everyone had things to do. They agreed to meet at the same Italian café at 7:00pm. Then Shelley went to visit her mother and Bill. Akina and Chrysa went shopping.

Jarmo and Pachai went out with Hehu. Hehu said he had a plan. He wouldn't tell Pachai and Jarmo about the plan. He said it was a surprise.

When Chrysa and Akina arrived at the café, the three men were already there.

"You had a successful afternoon," smiled Pachai when he saw how many bags Akina and Chrysa were carrying.

"Yes," answered Akina. "The shops here are very good. But I am so tired."

Chrysa and Akina sat down at the table and ordered water and fruit juice.

"What did you three do today?" asked Chrysa.

"Hehu took us horse riding!" said Pachai.

"Where did you go horse riding?" asked Chrysa. "We are in the city."

"There is a big park near here. It's called Centennial Park. It is popular for horse riding," explained Jarmo. "There is a school for people who want to learn to ride. One of Hehu's cousins works there. He rented us horses. I can ride a little, so Hehu's cousin found me a nice quiet horse and I didn't fall off."

"Did you enjoy riding, Pachai?" asked Akina. "It was your first time, wasn't it?"

"Hehu is a great teacher. I enjoyed it. I want to try again. I can go riding in the Bois de Boulogne in Paris."

"Shelley's late," said Jarmo. "Shall we wait for her? Or shall we order?"

As he finished speaking Shelley came into the restaurant. She looked around, and saw their table. "Sorry I'm late," she said as she arrived at the table. "Did you order yet?"

"Not yet." Pachai waved to the waitress, and she came to the table. After she took their orders and went away, Hehu said. "Did you have a nice afternoon?"

"Yes, I did. I only met Bill once before. It was nice to get to know him better."

"Do you like him?" asked Akina.

"Yes. He's very nice. He has a lot of money now, but I think when he was young, his life was very hard. He loves my mother very much. I'm sure he will make her happy."

The waitress arrived with big bowls of pasta and salads. While they ate, they told Shelley about their afternoons.

Back at the house, Akina and Chrysa took their shopping bags up to their bedroom. Shelley went too. "I want to see what you bought," she said. She sat on the bed, and Akina and Chrysa took their new dresses from their bags and showed her.

"Wow!" said Shelley. "You will both look amazing at the party." Then she took a small parcel out of her pocket.

"Bill gave this to me when I was leaving. He told me to wait until I got home before I opened it."

She untied the parcel. Inside, she found a folded piece of paper and a small box. She read the message on the paper. Then she gave it to Chrysa. Akina and Chrysa read it together.

--- *My company trades in oil and gas, but when I was a young man I hunted for opals. It was a hard life, but I was lucky, and I found enough opals to start my company. I never sold the first opal I found. It is large and beautiful. I asked a goldsmith to put it into a necklace for your mother. I will give it to her on Saturday.*

I spent my life in oil and gas fields all over the world. I never married, and I have no children. I was so lucky to meet your mother. And now I will have a stepdaughter too! I want you to have this small present from me. ---

Shelley opened the box. Inside the box was a pair of opal earrings. The stones shone in every colour of blue and green. They were beautiful.

"Look!" said Shelley. Akina and Chrysa looked inside the box.

"They're perfect!" said Chrysa. "They will match your party outfit so well!"

"What party outfit?" asked Shelley. "I don't know what I'm going to wear!"

Akina and Chrysa smiled at each other. "Well, we stayed at the beach house, and now we are staying here in your home," said Akina. "We expected to pay for a hotel, but we don't have to. So we have some extra spending money. Chrysa and I bought dresses, but we had some money left over. So we bought you a present!"

Chrysa opened another bag, and took out a bright blue top. It was made from shiny material, and had green and blue beads sewn around the v-shaped neckline.

"We think these colours are good for you," she said. "And we bought some pants to go with them." Akina held up a pair of white pants.

Shelley was excited. "I must try them on!" The clothes fitted perfectly. "How did you get the size right?" she asked.

"We're very good shoppers," said Akina proudly.

When they were eating breakfast the next morning, Chrysa asked, "What are you guys wearing to the party?"

"Chrysa! Don't worry!" laughed Jarmo. "We'll all look very smart!"

Chrysa didn't believe him. "Hehu. What will you wear?"

"My normal clothes," said Hehu. "No one will be looking at me."

"Not shorts!" shouted Chrysa. Everyone laughed. Hehu always wore shorts.

Hehu loved teasing Chrysa. She was so serious about clothes and fashion. He didn't tell Chrysa, but before horse riding, he had gone to a menswear shop, and bought a smart shirt and pants.

"Don't worry, Chrysa," said Pachai. "Shelley, Akina and you will all look beautiful. No one will look at us guys. Now, what shall we do today?"

They decided to go to Manly. They could swim, and have a picnic there. Jarmo searched on his iPad. "We can take a bus to Circular Quay, and then a boat ferry to Manly," he said.

"It would be fun to do something different tonight," said Shelley. "Why don't we go to the theatre?"

They found tickets for a musical called Georgy Girl. It started at 8:00pm.

"We'll have enough time to come back here and shower and change," said Shelley. "It's going to be a great day!"

6. BRISBANE

They left the house in Paddington early on Saturday morning and took a bus to Circular Quay and a train out to the airport. It was almost lunchtime when the plane landed at Brisbane airport. As they walked out into the terminal, they saw a man carrying a sign. It said

---Shelley Rakena ---

Shelley walked over to the man. "I'm Shelley Rakena," she said.

"Good," smiled the man. "I'm your driver. The limo is outside."

"Limo!" said Shelley. "What's happening?"

"Our company is very busy today. We are picking up all the out-of-town guests for Mr Curtis' yacht party. They are coming from all over Australia. Mr Curtis has reserved hotels for the out-of-town guests as well. Come this way."

The driver took them to a nice beachside hotel.

"It's going to be a big party," said the driver. "There was a story about it on the social page of the newspaper this morning. And one of the talk show hosts on radio was speaking about it. You are going to have a great time! I'll be back at six pm to take you to the yacht."

Pachai looked at his watch. "One o'clock," he said. "Let's check in, and then have some lunch."

They checked into the hotel, put their bags in their rooms, and then met by the main entrance. They walked out onto the street and saw an outdoor café.

"That looks nice," said Akina.

They ate sandwiches and drank juice while they watched people on the busy streets. Everyone was very casual and relaxed. They listened to the many tourists. They heard so many different languages.

"People come here from all over the world," said Shelley. "It is very popular."

After lunch they took a walk along the beachfront, then went back to the hotel. Pachai, Jarmo and Hehu planned to go swimming.

"Make sure you leave enough time to get ready for the party," said Chrysa.

"Ten minutes!" laughed Hehu.

7. PARTY TIME!

They met in the hotel lobby at 5:45 pm.

"Wow!" said Jarmo. "You all look great!"

"Do you think so?" laughed Shelley. She was wearing the blue and green top with white pants and high-heeled gold sandals. The opal earrings from Bill swung from her ears. They shone in the light as she moved her head.

Akina was wearing a short black lace dress with a wide skirt. The dress had a red belt. She looked very cute.

Chrysa's dress was long. It had narrow straps decorated with beads. The pale sea green suited her blonde hair, and lightly tanned skin.

"You guys look OK too," said Shelley.

Jarmo was wearing black as usual. Pachai's designer jeans looked great with one of his silky white shirts.

"Hehu!" said Chrysa. "I don't believe it! Where are your shorts?"

"Pachai hid them all," laughed Hehu. "He is scared of you! He thought you would be angry if I wore shorts."

Hehu was wearing a checked shirt and tan pants. They suited him. He always looked handsome, but tonight he looked especially good.

They waited in the lobby for the limousine to arrive.

"I like your earrings," Shelley said to Chrysa. "Are they real diamonds?"

"Oh, no," answered Chrysa. "I never pack my good jewellery when I travel. I might lose it. Or it might get stolen. These are just glass, but I like them."

The limousine driver came in the hotel door and waved to them. They climbed into the waiting limousine. Bill's luxury motor yacht was waiting at the mouth of the Brisbane River. The limousine stopped. They thanked the driver.

"I'll be here at one am," he said. "Enjoy the party!"

They walked across to the dock and looked up at the yacht.

"It looks like a wedding cake," said Akina. "It's so big too!"

The yacht had three levels. Each level had a deck at the back. The lowest deck was the largest.

"I guess that's the party deck," said Hehu.

Two men in white pants and red polo shirts were waiting at the gangway.

"Welcome!" said the older man. "I'm Chester. I'm the captain of this yacht, and this is Wally. I guess you are Barbara's daughter." He smiled at Shelley. "I hope you and your friends have a great time. Barbara and Bill are on the lower rear deck with their guests. Wally will take you there."

They followed Wally to the big lower deck at the rear of the boat. Jarmo could hear music. He looked up. A band was playing on the smaller deck above.

He looked around. There were thirty or forty people on the deck. They were all very smartly dressed. The women were all wearing beautiful dresses and a lot of jewellery.

Bill's friends are rich, thought Jarmo. *But then Bill is rich too.*

"Come and meet Mum and Bill," said Shelley. They walked over to where Bill and Barbara were standing. Barbara was wearing a beautiful opal and gold necklace.

"Mum, Bill," said Shelley. "These are my friends. Chrysa, Akina, Jarmo and Pachai. Bill, this is my cousin Hehu."

Everyone shook hands. "Thank you for inviting us," said Chrysa. "It was very kind of you."

"Thank you for coming," smiled Barbara. "Shelley likes you all so much. It is great for me to finally have a chance to meet you. And you girls look so pretty!"

"I'm wearing the earrings you gave me," Shelley said to Bill. "Thank you! They look good, don't they?"

"Yes, they do suit you," smiled Bill. "I'm so pleased you like them."

"It's an amazing yacht," said Pachai. "Perfect for a party. Do you spend much time on her?"

"In the past, I never had more than two or three weeks a year free to go cruising," answered Bill. "So I set up a yacht charter company. Most of the year, people hire the boat and crew. It's good because it pays for the cost of keeping the boat. But now, I am semi-retired, and I hope Barbara and I can take cruises together."

Chester, the captain, came over to Bill.

"Everyone has arrived now," he said. "We can leave. It will take about one hour to travel to Bribie Island. We will anchor there for about four hours, and then come back. Is that OK?"

"Sure," said Bill. "That's fine. When the yacht is anchored, I hope you and the rest of the crew will come back to the party."

"Thank you," said Chester. "We'd like that. But I will have to leave one person on the bridge for security and safety. We don't want any accidents tonight!"

He smiled at everyone and went away.

The party was wonderful. Three waiters moved through the party guests carrying champagne and wonderful tasty snacks. The band played. Everyone was very friendly. The six friends enjoyed themselves very much.

The boat stopped near Bribie Island and anchored. Most of the crew members came out onto the big deck and joined the party.

The waiters put big plates of prawns, fish and salads on a table at one side of the deck.

"I've eaten so many snacks, I don't feel hungry," said Chrysa.

"I couldn't eat any more either," agreed Akina. "I need some exercise to make room for more food."

"It would be great to dance," said Shelley. "The band is very good. But there's no room here for dancing."

"We could go up to the deck on the top level," said Hehu. "Above the band."

"I'm still hungry!" said Jarmo.

"The food will be there for an hour or more," said Shelley. "You can come back down and eat later."

"OK," said Jarmo. "I'll come up now, but not for too long."

Shelley went to speak to her mother. She came back smiling.

"Mum says it's a great idea. She says maybe she and Bill can join us later. Mum loves to dance."

8. INVASION

They moved to the narrow metal stairs that connected the decks. When they got to the top deck they saw a small sign. It said

--- *Games deck. Please don't damage the wooden floor. Sports shoes only please.* ---

Everyone took their shoes off and walked out onto the deck. They looked towards Bribie Island.

"It's very dark out there," said Akina.

"There are no houses at this end of the island. It is a national park," explained Shelley.

Akina walked over to the rail of the boat and looked down into the water.

"What's that?" she asked.

Pachai stood next to her, and looked down. "I don't see anything," he said.

"I don't know. I thought I saw something dark. Some dolphins maybe?" said Akina. "It doesn't matter. Oh, I like the song the band is playing now. Let's dance!"

They enjoyed themselves dancing up on the top deck for a few minutes. Then suddenly the band stopped. Jarmo was nearest the band. He moved over to the front rail and looked down. Then he turned quickly, dropped to the floor and put his finger to his lips.

He signaled to the others to get down onto the wooden surface of the deck. The band was silent, but suddenly they heard frightened screams and men shouting.

Shelley, Pachai, Akina, Chrysa and Hehu crawled across to the railing. It had canvas curtains, but they could see between them.

It was terrifying. The musicians were standing with their hands in the air. Facing them was a man dressed in black. His face was covered with a black scarf. He was pointing a machine pistol at the band members.

They could not see all the lower deck, but they guessed there were armed men there as well. They could hear women crying and screaming. The male guests were shouting. They could see all the guests. They had their hands in the air. They couldn't see the crew members, or the gunmen.

"Shut up!" a voice shouted. The noise from the guests didn't stop. Suddenly there was a *tacka tacka tacka* sound from a gun. A woman screamed loudly.

"That was a warning! If you don't shut up, I will shoot someone," said the voice roughly. There was a scary silence from the deck below.

"My men will come to you, one by one. When they get to you, you can lower your hands. Take off all your jewellery and watches. I want your handbags, your wallets and your mobile phones too. Put everything into the bags. As soon as they're done, put your hands in the air again. If anyone tries anything, my men will shoot you."

They could hear someone crying softly, below them, and they could hear people moving around. They saw another man carrying a machine pistol. His face was covered. He walked up to an elderly woman. She lowered her arms. She tried to take her earrings off. She was shaking so badly, she couldn't do it. He pushed her to the floor. He pulled the earrings out of her ears and the necklace from around her neck. He picked up her handbag from the deck. Then he kicked her very hard in the head and chest.

Hehu started crawling backwards from the rail, very slowly and quietly. The others did the same thing. At the back of the top deck was a small lounge and bar. The doors were open. They crawled backwards into the lounge. When everyone was inside, Hehu closed the doors. Then he pointed to the bar. They crawled behind the bar, and sat on the floor.

"There are windows everywhere," he said softly. "We mustn't be seen."

"But Hehu," whispered Chrysa. "We can't hide. We have to help those people."

"We will," said Hehu.

Chrysa looked at his face. She had never seen Hehu look like that. He was always relaxed and smiling, but now his face looked like stone.

She looked at Shelley. Shelley face was white. Her eyes were full of tears. She was very frightened. "Mum," she whispered.

Hehu reached over and held Shelley's hands. "Aunty Barbara is never silly. She won't do anything stupid. She will be fine. We must make a plan. I am guessing our phones won't work here. Even if they do, these men will get away before the police can get here."

Shelley turned on her smartphone. She looked at the bars.

"No luck," she said. "There is no signal."

Hehu looked at Pachai and Jarmo. "We have a big advantage. The robbers don't know we are on this boat. The Captain said he would leave a crew member on the bridge. Can we get to the bridge from here?"

"What's the bridge?" asked Akina.

"Oh, it's like the main control room. It's where the captain sits and commands the boat," explained Hehu.

"I'll go and look," said Jarmo. "There's a door over there. I guess it goes to the rest of the yacht."

He crawled out from behind the bar and across the floor of the lounge. He stood up next to the door with his ear against the door. He shook his head, opened the door silently, and went out.

"Do you have any ideas?" Pachai asked Hehu.

"Not yet," he answered.

Pachai was looking at the windows along the sides of the lounge.

"We can't go back onto the deck," he said. "One of the gang might see us. We were lucky no one saw us out there before. Maybe we can climb out those side windows."

"We'll wait until Jarmo comes back," said Hehu.

They sat and looked at the door. They heard another round of firing, *tacka tacka tacka*. It seemed a long time, but finally Jarmo came back. He crawled across to them. He had a bag on his back.

"OK," he said. "The door to the bridge is locked, so I couldn't get in. But there is a window in the door. The crewman is lying on the floor. His hands and feet are tied with rope. The yacht has a closed circuit TV system. I could see the display screens through the window. The situation is not good on the lower deck. I could see a man lying on the floor. I think he was shot in the leg. There's a lot of blood. And the elderly woman. The one that guy kicked, is still lying on the floor. The robbers are collecting jewellery and money from the guests. It seems to be taking a long time.

"I counted four guys carrying guns. The one who is on the band deck, and three more on the lower deck. I didn't see any others."

"What is the layout of the boat?" asked Pachai. "Where can we go without the bad guys seeing us?"

"On this level there is the deck, this room, a small hallway and the bridge. There are steps from the hallway down to the next level. The next level is much bigger. There is another lounge like this one, and some cabins. Then the steps go down to the lowest deck where the party is. There's a big lounge, and I think maybe a kitchen and more cabins. The engine room and the crew's lounge and cabins are below that."

"What's in the bag?" asked Pachai.

Jarmo smiled. "I saw the crew's rooms on the closed circuit TV. I thought some of us aren't dressed for action. I went down to their cabins. I took some clothes. I found some rope too."

"Well done!" said Chrysa.

"Good," said Hehu. "Pachai and I are going outside. We will go out through the side windows. We know the robbers are on the lower deck, and the second deck. We'll climb over the railings and down to the lower deck."

Jarmo took a pair of engineer's overalls out of the bag and gave them to Pachai. Pachai pulled off his shirt and put on the overalls.

"I couldn't find anything to fit you, Hehu," Jarmo said. "Sorry."

"No problem," said Hehu. He picked up the rope from the floor and wound it around his waist. "I'll be fine like this. Ready, Pachai? I'll go along one side and you go along the other side. We'll meet at the front of the yacht."

Pachai nodded. They went to opposite sides of the lounge. Everyone held their breath while the two men struggled to open the wide windows and climb out.

They sat waiting for shouts or the sound of gunfire. But they didn't hear anything. Then Chrysa said, "Shelley. I have never seen Hehu like this before. He is very scary."

Shelley nodded. "He doesn't often get angry. He is usually very calm. But he is very angry tonight. When that horrible man kicked that woman, he got really mad. He hates violence, but if he has to attack someone, he will."

"And so will we," said Jarmo. "I'm going back through the door – maybe Hehu and Pachai will come back that way. Why don't you get changed?" He pointed to the bag.

A few minutes later, Chrysa was wearing a pair of engineer's overalls. Akina had changed into a long sleeved black T-shirt and shorts. The shorts were too big for her. She took the red belt from her dress and tied it around her waist. Shelley found a crew uniform in the bag.

Pachai and Hehu came through the door at the end of the lounge. Jarmo was with them.

"The robbers are very confident," said Pachai when he came in. "They think they have everything under control. All the guests are on the party deck with three of the robbers. They all have guns. The band is on the second deck with the fourth robber. There is the crew member locked inside the bridge. The rest of the yacht is empty. Hehu thinks we must hurry."

9. THE PLAN

"Do you have a plan?" asked Jarmo. "We are all ready to do anything."

Hehu sighed. "Yes. I have a plan, but it is very dangerous. I am worried. If anything goes wrong, you could get badly hurt, or killed."

"Hehu!" said Chrysa. She spoke quietly, but she sounded very strong and fierce. "Those men have hurt two people already! They might kill someone next! We can't hide and do nothing! It is not right!"

"OK, OK, Chrysa," said Hehu. "But everyone must agree."

"We do," said all the others.

"Well, this is my plan. There are six of us, but only four of them. But they have guns, and we don't. Our advantage is that they don't know we're here. We know they are not afraid to use their guns. So far they have only shot one person in the leg, but I'm sure they'll shoot at anyone who tries to stop them. We can't try to attack them on the lower deck. They will fire their machine pistols, and I am sure someone will be shot. The risk is too great.

"So Pachai and I think we should wait until they are ready to leave the yacht. We don't think they will tie everyone up. We think they will take hostages.

"The walkways along the sides of the yacht are narrow. They must go one person at a time. We can't attack four men with guns. So we will only attack two."

"How can that work?" asked Jarmo. "There will still be two men with machine pistols! It's crazy!"

Pachai smiled. "We will set a trap for the first two robbers. When I went along the side of the boat, I saw how they got onto the yacht. They have a very small, very fast boat. They came alongside the yacht, and they tied bamboo poles to rope ladders. The ladders have hooks at the top. They used the bamboo poles to push the ladders up until the hooks were over the deck railing. I could see the bamboo poles floating in the water. It is a clever way to get onto a much bigger boat."

"Akina. You are our best climber. Do you think you can climb down their ladders in the dark?" asked Hehu.

Akina said, "Of course I can."

"If you cut the ropes about two metres above the water, the first two robbers will be in trouble. They will fall into the water."

"But they can swim to the boat!" said Chrysa.

"Don't worry. I have a plan for that too," said Hehu. "Akina will do it."

"And the other two men?" asked Jarmo. "They might have a hostage."

"I agree," answered Hehu. "It will be dangerous and risky, but we have to attack them before they get to the ladders, and before they realise the ladders have been cut."

"So what do we do?" asked Shelley.

"I'll explain," said Hehu. He went to the bar and searched the shelves and drawers. He held up a small knife and tested it against his thumb. He gave it to Akina.

"It's not very good," he said. "I hope it is sharp enough to cut through the ropes on the ladders." He also found a bottle of detergent under the sink and gave it to her.

"Now this is what we must do."

Everyone listened carefully.

They went through the door at end of the lounge.

"Be very quiet," said Hehu. They followed Jarmo along a hallway, and down two stairways. They came out on the lowest walkway and went over to the railing. They looked down at the sea. It was very dark. The sea was black, but they could see the robbers' boat tied to the bottom of one of the ladders.

"Akina," said Hehu. "Are you OK? Can you do this?"

"Yes, I can," she said.

Pachai helped Akina climb over the rail. Then they watched while she climbed down very quickly. She pulled the robbers' boat towards the ladder and jumped.

"Where is she?" whispered Chrysa. "I can't see her!"

Pachai held Chrysa's shoulder. "There she is," he said.

Akina was on the boat. She was bending over something.

I hope she can get the cap off the fuel tank, thought Jarmo.

Finally, Akina turned back to the ladder and started climbing. When she was about two metres above the water she stopped. She held on with one hand and reached down below her feet. She was cutting the ropes of the ladder. Then she climbed back up. Pachai pulled her over the rail to where her friends were waiting. Her hands were bleeding.

"The knife is not very good," she said. "But I did it. The bottom of the ladder is no good. I left a little piece of rope on both sides. It will break as soon as anyone puts any weight on it. They will fall into the water."

"Could you put the detergent in the fuel tank?" asked Hehu.

"Yes," answered Akina. "No problem. Now I will cut the second ladder."

This time Akina was very quick. When she was back on the walkway, she gave her knife to Hehu. "You might need it," she said.

Then Akina and Shelley hurried quietly to the second floor of the yacht. Soon they were in the room behind the second deck. The room was dark. They walked quietly along the sides of the room to the glass door.

The band members were still standing with their arms in the air. The drummer thought he heard something behind him. He looked over his shoulder. He was surprised to see a young woman behind the glass door. She put her finger to her lips and disappeared.

Who is she? A member of the crew? I wonder what she thinks she can do? This is terrible! he thought.

Chrysa and Jarmo were waiting on the lowest walkway. There were two cabins with doors onto the walkway. They were standing in the doorways with their backs flat against the doors. Above them, Pachai and Hehu were sitting on the second deck railing.

They heard more shouting and the sound of the machine pistol being fired again.

I hope that's just another warning, thought Chrysa.

Shelley and Akina listened hard from inside the second floor lounge.

One of the robbers said, "We have hostages. Don't move. Don't do anything. We will kill the hostages if you do."

Then the drummer waved his hand towards the door. Very slowly and carefully, Shelley went to the door and opened it. The drummer didn't turn around, but he said, "The guy with the gun has gone to the lower deck. Stay behind us."

Shelley and Akina went out onto the deck and stood behind the band members.

They heard the gang shouting at the guests. "Lie down on the floor. Put your hands on top of your heads. Don't move. If we see or hear anything, we'll kill the hostages!"

Back on the walkway, Chrysa and Jarmo could hear the shouting, but could not hear the words. They stayed very still.

Then they heard men talking. Two of the gang were walking towards them.

"Well, that was easy," laughed one of them. "These old rich people don't cause trouble."

"We'll be away from here in two minutes," said the other.

They walked to the railing and started climbing down the ladders.

It's all about timing, thought Pachai. *If the other robbers don't come soon, this plan won't work!*

A few seconds later, four more people appeared. One of the robbers was walking in front. He looked very relaxed. His gun was hanging from his shoulder. Behind him was Bill, carrying two big backpacks. He had one in each hand. Then came Barbara. Behind Barbara was the last robber.

Thank goodness Shelley isn't seeing this, thought Jarmo.

They heard shouting and a loud splash from the water below them.

"Now," shouted Hehu. The first man stopped in surprise. He looked up. Bill looked up too. He saw Pachai was about to jump. Very quickly, he swung the two backpacks forward, and hit the robber in front of him in the back of his legs. The robber fell down on his face. Pachai landed on the robber's back. Chrysa ran and took the machine pistol.

Bill and Chrysa looked back. Hehu was behind the second man. The man had his arm around Barbara's neck. Hehu held the man's arms, and pulled them backwards. The gun fell to the deck. The robber let go of Barbara. She ran towards Bill. Chrysa was still holding the machine pistol. She walked forward pointing it at the robber. Jarmo picked up the second gun and went to help Pachai.

Bill was hugging Barbara.

"Where are the other two?" he asked.

Jarmo pointed over the side of the yacht. Still holding Barbara, Bill walked to the rail. The two men were in the water. They were trying to get into their boat.

"They'll get away!" said Bill.

"I don't think so," said Hehu. "Akina put detergent in the fuel tank. The boat engine will start, but they won't go far before it breaks down."

Barbara looked at Hehu. "Shelley! Where's Shelley?"

"She's OK. She went with Akina to the lower deck. They will be helping the guests."

Hehu was still holding the robbers' arms behind his back, and Chrysa was pointing the gun at him.

Pachai and Jarmo pulled the other robber to his feet.

Then they heard Akina's voice. "Pachai, Pachai! Shelley says 'Come quickly!'" Akina was running towards them.

Bill went to help Jarmo hold the robber. Pachai ran past Akina towards the back of the boat.

"Why does Shelley want Pachai?" asked Barbara.

"He's a doctor," said Hehu. "Your guests need his help."

Chrysa and Barbara hurried after Pachai and Akina.

Hehu unwound the rope from around his waist. "Can we tie these guys up?"

They tied the robbers up and pushed them into a cabin. Bill locked the door.

"Now, we must get into the bridge and use the radio to contact the police," he said.

10. THE POLICE

On the deck, the guests were standing in small groups talking quietly. The band members were sitting together in one corner. The crew and waiters were standing around a man lying on the ground. Pachai was kneeling next to him holding a thick bandage against the man's leg.

"It's Chester," said Bill. "He tried to stop the robbers and they shot him."

"The young doctor checked him," said one of the waiters. "He has lost a lot of blood, but the doctor says he will be OK."

Bill spoke to the other crew members. The men nodded and disappeared.

"They are going to the bridge," said Bill. "I guess the door is locked, but they will break it open if they have to. We can contact the police by radio."

Shelley was kneeling next to the elderly woman who had been kicked, holding her hand. Akina and Chrysa had a first aid box. They were helping many of the guests who had cuts and bruises from being pushed and hit by the robbers.

"Are you all OK?" Barbara asked the waiters. "We're fine," said one of them.

"Then could you please make tea and coffee, and serve it in the lounge?"

All the guests and the band moved into the lounge and sat on the wide sofas and chairs.

Soon there were only a few people left out on the deck. One of the crew brought blankets for Chester and the injured woman. Another came down from the bridge and spoke to Bill.

"The police are coming by motor boat and helicopter. They are sending an ambulance helicopter for Chester and the woman."

It was very quiet on the deck. They could hear the guests speaking softly as the waiters served tea and coffee. Everyone was in shock.

Finally they heard the sound of helicopters. As the helicopters came closer the noise was very loud. The ambulance helicopter hovered over the yacht while two paramedics were lowered to the deck. A stretcher was then lowered from the helicopter.

The paramedics spoke quickly to Pachai. They lifted Chester onto the stretcher and he was lifted up into the air. The stretcher came back down to pick up the elderly woman.

Pachai came over to where the others were standing.

"Will they be OK?" asked Bill.

"I think so. I hope so," answered Pachai.

Next, the police were lowered from the second helicopter.

"Everyone, please wait in there," said one of the first policemen to arrive. He pointed to the lounge. "We will come and talk to you soon."

Bill, Barbara, the crew and the six young people joined the guests in the lounge. It seemed a long time, but finally four policemen came in.

"Can we talk to you, Sir," they said to Bill.

Bill went out with two of the policemen. The other two policemen started to go around the room. They talked to every guest. They asked for names and addresses. They wanted to hear everyone's story.

A policeman came into the room and asked the young people to go with him. He took them to the lounge on the second deck. The police had made a temporary office.

"Please sit down," said a senior policeman sitting behind a table. He asked them to tell their stories.

When everyone had finished talking, he said, "What you did was very dangerous. Why did you do it?"

"We thought the gang would take a hostage. Maybe more than

one," said Hehu. "We thought they might kill the hostages when they got away. We didn't want that to happen. So we took the risk."

The policeman looked at the six young people. *They were very brave,* he thought. *It's hard to believe what they did.*

"You might have been killed," he said.

"Yes," said Chrysa. "That's true. But other people might have been killed. We thought we must do it."

The policeman looked at Chrysa. She looked very strange. She was still wearing the engineer's overalls, but she had forgotten to take her earrings out. The glass beads shone in the light.

And that other young woman, he thought. *The one they call Akina. She climbed down the rope ladders in the dark. She got onto the gang's boat and sabotaged the engine.*

"Our police boat has arrested the two robbers who escaped, and you captured the other two," he said. "We know all these men. They are members of a very clever and dangerous gang. They have targeted society events before. They must have heard about the party, and decided it was a good chance. All the valuables they took were in the bags we found on the deck. So I think we should say 'thank you'. But please, never do such a dangerous thing again!"

11. TIME TO LEAVE

Finally the police said the crew could take the yacht back to Brisbane. Some policemen stayed on the yacht. Bill went up to the bridge. Barbara went with him. They wanted to be together.

Jarmo collected plates of food and some cans of drink. He took them up to the second level lounge. The others were waiting there.

"I asked the band to join us," he said. "They didn't get any supper."

The sun was rising when the yacht finally arrived in Brisbane. They stood by the rails and watched as the exhausted passengers got off the boat. Some went away by ambulance. No one was badly hurt, but some guests were suffering from shock. Others climbed into limousines.

Barbara and Bill came to join them.

"Thank you," said Bill. He shook hands with Pachai, Hehu and Jarmo. He kissed Chrysa and Akina. Then he hugged Shelley. "I always wanted a daughter. Now I have one, but I might have lost you!"

Barbara smiled at them all. "You are really amazing. It is terrible that Chester was hurt, but it could have been much worse. Bill and I were very afraid the robbers would kill us as soon as they got away."

"Will you please come and stay with us in Sydney?" asked Bill. "I want to get to know you better."

"Uh, thank you, but not this time," said Jarmo. "We have to go to the police station today. So we will get back to Sydney much later than we planned. Then tomorrow night, we must all fly home. Our holiday has finished, and it's time to go."

"Next time you're in Australia, then," said Bill. "Where's your limo?" he asked. "You will want to go to your hotel and get some rest before you go to the police station."

"They are taking all the older guests first. And they needed extra cars to take some people to the hospital," said Shelley. "They will send a car for us as soon as they can."

"I want to take Barbara back to the hotel. We will have to stay here in Brisbane for a few days while everything is fixed up. So we'll say goodbye. "

"See you in a few days, Mum," said Shelley hugging her mother.

"Thank you again," said Bill shaking hands with everyone.

They stood and watched while Bill helped Barbara off the yacht and into a waiting car. They waved as the car drove away.

"Well," said Jarmo. "That was quite a party!"

The others laughed. "We've never had a quiet, simple holiday," said Chrysa. "But when you come to Greece, we will just have fun. There won't be any excitement or drama."

"No excitement, no drama sounds great to me," Shelley yawned. "The only thing I know right now it that I want to sleep."

"Eat, then sleep," said Jarmo.

"OK, OK! We'll eat, then sleep." Shelley took Jarmo's arm. "Look! There's our limo. Let's go."

Pachai took Chrysa's arm and they followed Shelley and Jarmo.

"I can't believe we're flying home tomorrow," said Pachai.

"And then, the next time we all meet, will be in Athens. I can't wait!" said Chrysa.

DEATH ON AN ISLAND

1. DIMITRIS IS INTERESTED

Dimitris Papadakis works on the front desk of a small hotel in Athens. He is very good at his job, because he is very interested in people. He likes meeting new people and chatting with them. He is interested in their lives. He is interested in their clothes, their jobs, and their families. He dreams that one day he will be able to travel to other countries, but his salary is low, so it is difficult to save money for travel.

One Tuesday in July, Dimitris was at work. It was late morning and it was quiet. It was the time between check-out and check-in. The cleaning crews were very busy, and so were the chefs and kitchen staff. But Dimitris had nothing to do. So he was enjoying watching the people in the lobby.

A taxi arrived in front of the wide glass entrance doors. A tall, elegant, handsome man in a white shirt and jeans got out. He was carrying a travel bag. Dimitris waited for him to come to the front desk.

I wonder who he is? thought Dimitris. He looked at the reservations for the day, but he couldn't guess. *He looks like he might be Indian, but I can't see an Indian name on the list.*

The man didn't come to the front desk. He looked around the lobby. Then he looked at his watch. The coffee shop was empty. He sat down at one of the tables near the entrance.

He's waiting for someone, thought Dimitris.

Then a man and woman with backpacks came into the lobby. The man was very big. He was wearing a T-shirt and shorts. He had brown skin and black hair. He looked strong and fit.

He looks like an athlete, thought Dimitris.

The woman was small. She was wearing denim shorts and a very bright blue shirt. She had short red hair. She was smiling. She looked very excited. She looked around the lobby. Then she saw the man in the coffee shop.

"Pachai!" she shouted, pointing to the man in the coffee shop. The man in the white shirt stood up and walked over to her. He shook hands with the man and hugged the woman. They were laughing and talking. They were very pleased to see each other.

The man in the white shirt is called Pachai, thought Dimitris. *There are no names like that on the check-in list. I wonder if they will stay here in the hotel?*

Soon guests started arriving to check in, and Dimitris was busy. The coffee shop was full. It was after 2:30pm before Dimitris was free to look around the lobby and watch people.

He was surprised to see that Pachai and his friends were still at the same table. And now there were two more people with them. A tiny woman with long black hair, dressed in pink, was chatting to the red-haired woman. They were laughing. The man in the white shirt, Pachai, and the man who looked like an athlete were standing behind a small, very blond man dressed in black. The small man had an iPad on the table, and the three of them were looking down at the screen. The men looked serious.

The man in black said something, and the two other men sat down. The five young people started talking. It seemed like a meeting. They looked at their smartphones. They looked at the iPad. The small red-haired person was shaking her head. She was waving her hands.

Dimitris was very interested.

Those people all look so different. But I am sure they are very good friends. I wish I had international friends. But it seems something is wrong. I wish I could hear what they are saying.

Then the three men stood up and came to the front desk.

"Excuse me," said Pachai. "Is English OK?"

"Of course," answered Dimitris proudly. "How can I help you?"

"Do you have any messages for Pachai Mehta?"

Dimitris checked all the messages on his computer. "No. I'm sorry. There are no messages for that name."

"How about Jarmo Virtanen or Hehu Rakena?" asked Pachai.

Dimitris checked again. "No. I'm sorry. There are no messages for those names either."

The small blonde man spoke to the other men. "Maybe Chrysa left a message for Shelley or Akina." He turned back to Dimitris. "Could you please look for Shelley Rakena or Akina Tanaka?"

"Nothing," answered Dimitris. "But Chrysa? Would that be Chrysa Melias?"

"Yes. That's right," said the small blonde man.

"Well, Chrysa Melias reserved the two suites on the top floor. Her father owns this hotel. We are looking forward to having Ms Melias stay with us."

Dimitris was a little worried. *Maybe I shouldn't have told them that. Maybe I will be in trouble.*

"Oh. Those will be our rooms," said Pachai. "Can we check in?"

"But Sir! There are no names on the reservations! I can't give you those suites!"

"Have a look on your iPad, Jarmo," said the third man. "You must have emails from Chrysa about this hotel and the reservations."

The blonde man put his iPad on the front desk and opened an email folder. He showed Dimitris an email. The email gave the hotel name and address. It said

---I have booked two suites on the top floor. Don't worry. We will get a good discount so they will not be so expensive! I will meet you in the lobby on Thursday morning. I will be there about 11:00am. Love Chrysa ---

Dimitris was now very worried. *If this is a lie, I will lose my job,* he thought. *But if it is true, then the hotel owner's daughter will be very angry. I might lose my job anyway.*

"Can you call Ms Melias?" he asked. "If I can talk to her, maybe it will be OK."

"We tried," said Pachai. "Her phone is turned off. We tried texts and email too. We don't know where Chrysa is. But I guess she got caught up in a traffic jam, or maybe something delayed her. I know it is difficult for you. Maybe you can talk to the hotel manager?"

Dimitris went away from the front desk. He was gone for twenty minutes. Pachai, Hehu and Jarmo waited at the front desk. Shelley and Akina watched from the coffee shop. Finally Dimitris came back.

"It's OK. I can give you the rooms. My manager called Mr Melias. He couldn't talk to him, but he spoke to Mr Melias' secretary. The secretary said that Chrysa reserved the suites for herself and five friends who were visiting Athens. I hope you are the five friends!"

"We are!" smiled the blond man. He waved to the two young women, and they came to the front desk.

They are so interesting, thought Dimitris. He watched carefully as they filled in the check-in forms. *The blond man is Jarmo Virtanen. He's from Finland. The tiny black-haired woman is Akina Tanaka. Japanese passport, but her address is in the USA. Pachai Mehta, Indian passport, address in Paris. Two people with the family name Rakena. Different passports, one Australian and one New Zealand. Two different home addresses. Not husband and wife then. Brother and sister? How did all these people meet? How do they know the Melias family? Why are they here?*

Dimitris handed over the access cards.

"Are you here for business?" he asked.

"No, no!" laughed Shelley Rakena. "We're here to have fun!"

2. SHALL WE TELEPHONE?

The suites on the top floor of the hotel were amazing. They had balconies with wonderful views of the Acropolis. Each suite had a living space, two bedrooms and two bathrooms.

Shelley and Akina put their bags in the larger bedroom of their suite.

"We will have to share a bed again," said Shelley. "But this one is huge!"

Akina laughed. "It's so wide, I'll have to use my phone to talk to you!"

"I hope Chrysa is happy in the smaller bedroom," said Shelley.

"I am sure she will be OK. It's a very nice room. But where is she?" Akina was worried.

Shelley was putting clothes into a drawer. She stopped and looked at Akina.

"I don't know. And I am worried too. Chrysa is never late. Chrysa sends text messages and emails all the time. But if she lost her iPhone and her car broke down, she wouldn't be able to contact us."

There was a knock on the door of the suite. Akina went to open it. It was Jarmo, Pachai and Hehu.

They came into the living area and sat down on the sofas.

Shelley came out of the bedroom to join them.

"What are we going to do?" asked Akina. "I am very worried."

"When was the last time any of us heard from Chrysa?" asked Pachai.

Everyone looked at their smartphones. Jarmo looked at his iPad too.

"Chrysa sent the same emails to all of us. The emails were about this hotel and her plans for sightseeing. But she sent some personal messages too. I got an email the day before I left Helsinki. She wanted to remind me the sun in Greece is very strong. I should have a sunhat."

"I got a message while I was in San Francisco airport," said Akina. "It was about clothes."

Everyone smiled. Chrysa and Akina loved fashion.

"Everyone please tell me the date, time and where you were, when you last had a message from Chrysa," said Jarmo.

Everyone told him and Jarmo calculated everything to the same time zone.

"OK," he said. "Chrysa has not communicated with any of us for forty-six hours!"

"What?" shouted Shelley. "But she is living with her parents! She planned to leave their house early this morning to drive to Athens! My idea about a car breakdown and a lost iPhone is wrong. What has happened?"

"I think we should call her parents," said Akina. "She might be sick. She might have had an accident."

"But her parents would know," said Jarmo.

"Yes," answered Akina. "But they might not know how to contact us."

"We should be careful," said Pachai.

"Why?" asked Shelley.

"Mmmm. You know that Chrysa comes from a very strict family. Her parents want her to marry. They are not happy when she goes traveling alone. They want her to stay home and learn to be a good wife. They might not be happy that she has crazy international friends. So maybe they don't know about us. We might cause trouble for her if we call her family."

"But when the hotel manager called Chrysa's father, the secretary knew about this hotel reservation." Jarmo didn't understand.

"But the secretary said for Chrysa's friends. Maybe her parents think the suites were for Greek friends. Her girlfriends from school or university. A reunion or a shopping trip," said Pachai.

"OK. But we have to do something!" Shelley was talking very loudly. "She might be sick or kidnapped or in danger!"

"Calm down, Shelley," said Hehu. "We will do something. I have an idea."

Everyone turned to look at Hehu. Hehu is a very big and strong man. But he is very calm and gentle. He doesn't talk much, but when he speaks, everyone listens.

"What are Chrysa's hobbies? What does she do? I know she studies languages. Chrysa and I have been taking distance-learning classes together. We are studying Spanish. But that won't work for my idea. What else does she do?"

"Shopping," said Akina. "She goes shopping often. She comes to Athens to buy clothes and accessories. She likes going to restaurants and bars too. But I don't understand why you want to know."

"I'm going downstairs," said Hehu. "Try emailing Chrysa again while I'm gone."

Hehu went out the door. "What is Hehu going to do?" asked Pachai.

"No idea," answered Jarmo. "But I'll try another email."

Hehu came back about twenty minutes later.

"It's OK. Dimitris finishes work in about five minutes. He'll come up here then."

"Who's Dimitris?" asked Pachai.

"He's the guy from the front desk. He'll come up here and call Chrysa's parent's house when he finishes work. He'll ask to talk to Chrysa."

"But if Chrysa's not there, someone might ask 'Who is calling? Can I take a message?'" said Pachai "What will Dimitris say then?"

"He'll say he is calling about a bag she ordered," said Hehu.

"Hehu, that's a lie," said Shelley. "I don't like doing this. And maybe Dimitris will get into trouble."

"I know, Shelley. I don't like it either. But think about it. Pachai thinks it's a bad idea for us to telephone. He thinks it might make trouble for Chrysa. None of us can speak Greek. So if we call, we have to speak in English. With this plan, if Chrysa is there, we can talk to her. If she isn't there, at least we will know something."

"OK," said Shelley. "But I don't want Dimitris to get into trouble."

"I think it will be OK. I said he could call from Jarmo's iPad. I said we would give him a tip. He wants to do it."

Dimitris finished work at 4:00pm. He went to the locker room. He was thinking about his conversation with Hehu.

No one must know I made the phone call. If the manager finds out, I will lose my job. But if Mr Melias' daughter is in trouble and I help her, Mr Melias will be very pleased. I might get a bonus or a promotion. I will take the risk. But how can I go to the top floor suites? Front desk staff never go upstairs. It will be terrible if one of the cleaning staff sees me.

Then he had an idea. He hurried back to the front desk. Vasilis, who worked the evening shift, was talking to some guests. Dimitris quickly took an access card from under the desk. He walked into the manager's office.

"One of the people staying in the suites on the top floor left their access card in the lobby. I'll take it up to him before I go home."

The manager looked up from his computer. "Thank you, Dimitris. That would be very helpful."

Everyone was waiting for Dimitris in Shelley and Akina's suite. Jarmo had the iPad open on the desk. Dimitris sat down in front of the iPad.

"I found Chrysa's home telephone number through the Internet," said Jarmo. "I have entered it on Skype. The speakers are on. When someone answers the telephone, we will be able to hear. Just click on the telephone icon."

Dimitris clicked on the icon. Everyone was listening. They could hear the telephone ringing. Then a woman answered. It was not Chrysa's voice.

Dimitris spoke very quickly in Greek. The woman answered. Dimitris asked another question. The woman laughed and said something. Pachai heard the name Athena, and later he heard Thera. Dimitris said 'efcharistó', and pushed the red disconnect symbol.

"What did she say?" asked Pachai.

"It was very strange," answered Dimitris. "It was the maid who answered the phone. Chrysa wasn't there, and Mrs Melias was out. She said that Chrysa is away on vacation. I asked if I could contact Chrysa in Athens. She said 'no'. She said Chrysa is on a romantic vacation with her fiancé. She said Chrysa is on the island of Thera. You probably know this island. It is usually called Santorini."

Everyone started talking at once.

"Just a minute, everyone," said Hehu. "Dimitris shouldn't stay here too long. Thank you, Dimitris. You were very helpful."

He walked to the door with Dimitris. Hehu gave Dimitris some money. Then Dimitris went out, and Hehu closed the door.

"Wow!" laughed Akina. "That was a surprise! Chrysa plans to get married. I guess she forgot about us because she was so excited!"

Pachai was standing with his back to the door. "No!" he said. "Something is very wrong. The story is not true. I know it is not true!"

3. SURPRISE VISITORS

Hehu walked over to Pachai and patted him on the shoulder.

"Why don't we go out for a drink and a meal? We are all tired. I agree the story seems strange, but we are too tired to think about it properly."

"You're right, Hehu," said Pachai. "Let's eat, drink and sleep. Then we can think more clearly."

They went to a small restaurant near the hotel. It was cheap, and the food was good. Shelley and Pachai ordered grilled cheese, and the others ate lamb gyro. The meal was served with flatbread, sauces and delicious salads. No one talked very much. They were all very tired, and it seemed strange to be together without Chrysa.

Finally Pachai said, "I know we're tired. I know we can't do anything until tomorrow. But I want to explain why I think there is something wrong."

"OK," said Jarmo. "We all know you are very worried. So please tell us what you think."

Pachai took a deep breath. "We are all good friends. We all know Chrysa well. But I think Chrysa has told me more about her life. Last year, when Jarmo's mother died, Chrysa and I travelled to Helsinki together. We talked a lot on the plane. We both have the same problem. Our families want us to marry. My mother is looking for a good wife for me. I do not want to marry yet, but I must obey my family. Next year I will return to India and marry.

"Chrysa's family would like her to marry a guy called Michalis. She has known Michalis all her life. He is the son of her father's oldest friend. Her mother thinks it is a good marriage. Michalis has asked Chrysa's father for permission to marry her. Her father thinks it is a wonderful idea. There has been a lot of pressure.

"Chrysa doesn't want to marry Michalis. She wants to have a job. She wants to travel. Meet new people. Make new friends. She wants to marry in the future, but not now. Chrysa is very strong. I am sure she would not suddenly agree to marry some man."

"Maybe it's Michalis," said Shelley. "She has known him all her life. Maybe she suddenly realised that she loved him."

"She does not love Michalis," said Pachai. "Chrysa did not say a lot. But she does not like him. She does not trust him. She sees him often, because he goes to the same parties. She is polite, but she doesn't want to be close to him."

"So, maybe Chrysa met a new man. She fell in love at first sight." Akina smiled. "It is very romantic."

"I don't believe it. I agree with Pachai. It's a bit strange," said Jarmo. "Chrysa didn't say anything to any of us about a new man in her life. She was still planning this vacation two days ago. She was so excited. She wanted us to have a wonderful time in Greece."

"Chrysa is not the kind of woman who forgets about her friends." Hehu was speaking. "But we can't do anything tonight. We should go back to the hotel and get some sleep." Hehu stood up and waved to the waiter to bring the bill.

When they walked into the lobby of their hotel, the manager ran towards them. He looked very excited and worried at the same time.

"You have visitors! They are waiting for you upstairs. They are in the ladies' suite!"

"What!" said Jarmo loudly. "You let strangers into the girls' suite! That was very wrong."

"No, no!" said the manager. He was trying to push them all towards the elevators. "They are not strangers! It is Mr and Mrs Melias. The owner of the hotel and his wife! They have come to see you!"

The elevator doors opened and they all crowded into the elevator. The manager got in too. When the elevator stopped at the top floor, the manager ran to the suite door and knocked on it. Then he opened it.

"Mr Melias. I am so sorry you had to wait. Here they are!"

Chrysa's parents were sitting on one of the big sofas. Chrysa's father stood up and walked towards them. He was quite short, but he looked strong. "I am Georgios Melias. This is my wife, Sofia. I'm sorry. My wife does not speak English."

He shook hands with Pachai, Jarmo and Hehu. Sofia Melias smiled at everyone from her place on the sofa.

"My manager told me your names. And you are friends of my daughter Chrysa?"

"Yes," said Pachai. "That's right. We came to Greece to visit her. She wanted to show us her country."

"I see," said Mr Melias. "I was surprised when my secretary told me about the phone call from my hotel manager. I was surprised Chrysa did not tell you her exciting news. Of course her plan to marry Michalis Dimas is very new. We are delighted. He is the son of my oldest friend. His father, Spiros Dimas died late last year.

"We Greeks are very polite people. We are kind to strangers. My daughter was wrong to invite you to come to Greece, and then not be here to greet you. My wife and I are very sorry. Please forgive Chrysa. She is young and in love. Love makes people forgetful.

"My wife and I came to apologise. I want you to be my guests in this hotel. There will be no charge for these rooms. Please stay as long as you want. My wife has brought some gifts for you."

He pointed to the coffee table. The table was covered in boxes of sweet pastries, wine bottles and flowers.

"Thank you!" said Shelley. "You are very kind. But is Chrysa OK? When will we see her?"

"I don't think you will see her," said Mr Melias. "Michalis took her to stay with his great-grandmother. She will stay there for maybe two or three weeks. The great-grandmother's house is on the island of Santorini. It is far from here. When Chrysa returns, she will email you. Please enjoy our beautiful country."

He turned to his wife. "Come," he said. Mrs Melias stood up. She smiled and bowed to everyone. Then she followed her husband out of the room.

The hotel manager was still standing by the door. He smiled nervously and went out, shutting the door.

Everyone sat down. "Wow," said Shelley. "That was interesting!"

"Chrysa looks exactly like her mother!" said Akina. "Beautiful clothes too. That white suit was perfect."

Jarmo looked at Pachai. "What do you think, Pachai? Do you still think there is a problem?"

"I don't know," Pachai answered. "If Chrysa's parents think everything is OK, then I guess she is safe. But I wonder if there was so much pressure from her family, that Chrysa gave up her own plans. Maybe she is safe, but I hope she is happy too."

"I am so tired," said Shelley yawning. "Will you guys please go away, so that Akina and I can get some sleep?"

4. SOFIA'S STORY

Everyone slept very late the next morning. Akina woke up when the telephone rang.

I guess the guys are awake, and want to go out for breakfast, she thought.

She turned over on the bed and picked up the telephone.

"It's too early," she said.

"I am Sofia Melias," said the voice on the other end of the phone line. "I am sorry. My English is not good, but I must talk to you."

Akina sat up quickly. "Yes, Mrs Melias. This is Akina. I can talk to you. What do you want to say?"

"Can you meet me? There is a coffee shop near the hotel. It's called Lattette. It is in the centre of Syntagma Square."

"Of course, I will meet you," said Akina. "Shelley will come too. What time?"

"Can you meet me in twenty minutes?" asked Mrs Melias.

"Akina looked at her smartphone. It was 10:15am. "I will try," said Akina. "I will hurry."

"Thank you," said Mrs Melias.

Akina looked across the bed at Shelley. Shelley was sleeping with a pillow over her head. Akina jumped up and ran around to other side. She pulled the pillow away from Shelley's head. "Wake up Shelley! Wake up now!"

"Waaah!" Shelley sat up holding her head. "What's the problem?"

"Get up! Hurry! We have to meet Chrysa's mother in twenty

minutes!"

Shelley jumped out of the bed and ran to the bathroom. "Why?" she shouted.

"I don't know but we must go."

Akina drank a glass of water and pulled on jeans and a T-shirt. Shelley came out of the bathroom and started looking for clothes. Akina used the bathroom. She washed her face and cleaned her teeth.

In five minutes they were out of the suite, and waiting for the elevator.

"Mrs Melias telephoned," said Akina. "We will meet her in a coffee shop near here."

"Shall we tell the guys? Maybe they should come too," said Shelley.

The elevator arrived and Akina pushed the button for the lobby.

"We don't have enough time. And maybe Mrs Melias doesn't want to talk to them."

"OK," said Shelley. "I'll send a text message to Hehu, and tell him we have gone out for coffee."

As they walked quickly through the lobby, Akina was looking at the map app on her phone. "I've found the coffee shop on the map. I think it is about ten minutes' walk from here."

The coffee shop was small. But when they walked in, they couldn't see Mrs Melias. Then a woman wearing a headscarf and sunglasses waved to them. She was sitting at a table towards the back of the room. As they walked over to the table, Mrs Melias took off her sunglasses. She looked tired and unhappy. She wasn't wearing any makeup. She looked very different from the elegant woman they had met the night before.

"Thank you for coming," she said slowly. "Please sit down. I have ordered coffee and pastries. I hope you like Greek coffee."

"Yes we do," said Shelley. "Chrysa taught us how to make it. She gave us all a special pot for making Greek coffee. Is it called a briki?"

Mrs Melias smiled. "Yes, that's right. You are Chrysa's friends. I am so worried about her. I want to tell you why I am worried."

Mrs Melias spoke very slowly, but her English was clear and easy to understand.

I wonder why her husband said she didn't speak English, thought Akina.

The coffee arrived. It was very strong and sweet. Mrs Melias picked up her cup and looked at the foam on top.

"My husband does not know I am here. I will have to get back to our house soon. I have a lot to say to you, and I must hurry. First I must tell you about my husband. It is important that you understand.

"He is a very good man. He is very strong and honest. He loves Chrysa very much, but he is traditional. Spiros Dimas was his oldest friend. Since Michalis and Chrysa were babies, their fathers hoped that they would marry. When Spiros was dying, he told my husband that his greatest wish was for Michalis and Chrysa to marry. My husband promised Spiros that it would happen.

"So you understand how important it is to my husband. He wants to keep his promise. Michalis wants to marry Chrysa, but she is not interested. I don't think she likes Michalis. I am sure she doesn't love him."

"What do you think, Mrs Melias?" asked Shelley.

"In the beginning, I thought it was a good idea. Michalis and Chrysa grew up together. They had the same life. The family culture is the same. It would be easy to live together. And the Dimas family is rich. I thought that was important.

"But then I started to change my mind. I saw that Chrysa was bored and unhappy. When she was planning to take a trip, she was excited and energetic. When she came back she would be happy. After a few days or weeks she would be quiet again. I saw she tried to stay away from Michalis.

"My husband thinks travelling to different countries is bad for Chrysa. He doesn't want her to have international friends. He doesn't want her to have modern ideas. He wants a nice, quiet, Greek daughter. He wants a daughter who would marry Michalis, have many children, and live happily in her hometown.

"After Spiros Dimas died, my husband put a lot of pressure on Chrysa. I was worried. I started watching Michalis. I saw him at parties. I saw that he drank a lot. I heard that he gambled. I thought he would not be a good husband for Chrysa."

"Did you tell your husband?" asked Akina.

"Of course. I tried, but Georgios would not listen to me."

"But Chrysa changed her mind," said Shelley. "Maybe she loves Michalis, or maybe she wants to please her father."

"No!" said Mrs Melias. "That is why I wanted to talk to you. You are her friends. You must help me! You must help my daughter!"

"But what's wrong?" asked Akina.

"Georgios and I went to Karvala to visit some friends. We were away for two days. Chrysa didn't want to go. She wanted to stay and plan for your visit. She told me all about you. She told me you were coming to Greece. She was very happy and excited. She did not tell her father. Georgios did not want Chrysa to have an international life. He thought the hotel bookings were for Chrysa's girlfriends. Her Greek girlfriends. When the hotel manager called, I told Georgios about you. He was not happy. But he is a good man. He did not want you to have a bad time in Greece.

"When we were travelling back from Karvala, Georgios got a phone call. It was from Michalis. Michalis told my husband that he and Chrysa spent the weekend together. He had asked Chrysa to marry him, and Chrysa had said 'yes'.

"Michalis said his great-grandmother is very ill. Maybe she will not live very long. He wanted her to meet Chrysa. So Michalis and Chrysa were taking a plane to Santorini. Chrysa wanted to help. She wanted to look after the old lady, so she would stay there for a while.

"Georgios wanted to talk to Chrysa, but Michalis said she was busy packing. Georgios was so pleased! His dream had come true. I thought it was strange. Why didn't Chrysa call us? But Georgios won't listen to me. He is planning a big engagement party and a big wedding."

"Do you know where the great-grandmother lives? Can you call her house?" asked Shelley.

"I tried. The telephone at the house is not working."

Akina looked at Mrs Melias. She looked so unhappy. Akina held her hand.

"I am sure she is OK. Please don't worry."

Mrs Melias held Akina's hand tightly. "I don't think Chrysa is OK. There are too many things that I don't understand."

She let go of Akina's hand and took her handbag from the back of her chair. She opened the bag and took out a piece of paper.

"My English is not good. I thought maybe I couldn't explain. So I made a list of phrases and translated them into English."

Mrs Melias put the paper on the table. Akina and Shelley read it.

… Chrysa didn't call.
Her iPhone was in her bedroom. She always keeps her iPhone with her.
She could use Michalis' phone. Why didn't she call?
I checked her clothes. She didn't pack anything. All her clothes, shoes and

accessories are in her room....

Shelley and Akina looked at each other.

"Can you talk to the police?" asked Shelley. "Or call someone in the neighbourhood, near the great-grandmother's house?"

Mrs Melias shook her head. "I wanted to do those things. I told my husband. He said 'no'. I was stupid. There was nothing wrong. I can't do anything. But you can. My husband can't stop you."

"We want to help," said Akina. "What can we do?"

Mrs Melias put her hand into her bag again. She took out another piece of paper and a lot of money. She put them in Akina's hand.

"I want you, and the young men to go to Santorini. I want you to find Chrysa!"

5. PLANS

Akina and Shelley walked back to their hotel. They didn't talk much. The meeting with Mrs Melias was so surprising. They were also worried.

Something is very wrong, thought Shelley. *I am sure Chrysa is in some kind of trouble.*

She took out her smartphone and sent a message to Hehu.

"I told Hehu to meet us in the coffee shop," she said to Akina.

Akina was holding her bag against her chest. She had all the money from Mrs Melias in it.

"OK," she said. "If we are going to search for Chrysa, I think we should start quickly."

When they arrived back at the hotel, Jarmo, Pachai and Hehu were in the coffee shop.

"Where did you two go?" asked Jarmo, waving his fork at them. "We've eaten an amazing breakfast. Well, brunch, I guess."

He looked at the clock on the wall. It was almost noon.

Shelley and Akina sat down.

"We went to meet Mrs Melias," said Shelley. "She called this morning. She wanted to talk to us."

"And?" asked Pachai. "Is she worried?"

"She is very worried," said Akina. "And we think she has good reason to be worried."

Shelley and Akina told Hehu, Pachai and Jarmo everything that

Mrs Melias had said.

"That's terrible!" said Pachai. "Chrysa has been kidnapped!"

"We don't know that," said Jarmo. "But something very strange is happening. Mrs Melias should call the police. Or call someone she knows on Santorini Island. Why isn't she doing something?"

Akina sighed. "Jarmo. It is very difficult for Mrs Melias. Her husband believes everything is OK. She came to see us in secret. She can't call the police. Her husband will know. He will tell the police that everything is perfect. His daughter is going to marry the man of her dreams."

"The man of her father's dreams you mean," said Shelley.

"Anyway, Mrs Melias can't ask anyone she knows to help her. So she has asked us to find Chrysa," said Akina.

"OK," said Hehu. "We will help her. We will work together, the way we always do. We will find Chrysa."

"It will be expensive to go to Santorini. Do we have enough money?" asked Jarmo.

"Ooh! I forgot," said Akina. She put her bag on the table and pulled out the money.

"Mrs Melias gave us this!"

"Put it away!" Shelley took the money and pushed it back into Akina's bag. "Someone will see it!"

"What's this?" asked Pachai. He picked up a piece of paper.

"Mrs Melias gave that to us too," answered Akina. "It is all the information about the great-grandmother. Her name and address, and a map. Her house is far from the main towns and villages on Santorini."

"We have everything we need," said Hehu. "When can we leave here and go to Santorini?"

Jarmo switched on his iPad and started searching.

"We can travel by boat or plane. We will need a rental car…"

Hehu got up and walked across to the front desk. Dimitris was watching them. Dimitris was wondering what was happening. He was very pleased when he realised that Hehu wanted to talk to him.

When Hehu returned to the coffee shop, Jarmo said, "We have everything organised. It would be wonderful to go to Santorini by boat, but this is an emergency. So we will take a plane at six twenty-five pm. We have reserved a rental car. Pachai will drive it."

"That's quick work," said Hehu. "But we'll need something else as well," said Hehu.

"A hotel?" asked Jarmo.

"Of course, a hotel," said Hehu. "But I talked to Dimitris. He says that there will be many English speakers in the main towns, at the airport, and at restaurants. But people as old as Michalis' great-grandmother seldom speak English. None of us speak Greek. I think we'll need an interpreter. Dimitris does not work tomorrow or the next day. I think we should ask him to come. Of course we must pay him."

"Can't we get an interpreter when we arrive on Santorini?" asked Shelley.

"I don't think we can get an interpreter immediately," said Pachai. "We will be arriving late. If we hire a car with a driver, the driver will speak English, but I don't think that is a good idea. The driver will talk to other people. The Melias family and the Dimas family are very rich. The driver might talk to the newspapers. Dimitris has good reasons not to tell anyone. The Melias family owns this hotel. Hehu always has good ideas."

"What if Mr Melias finds out? He will be very angry. Dimitris could lose his job," Akina was worried.

"Well, Dimitris says front desk clerks often take guide jobs in their free time. It is a good way to make money. If Mr Melias doesn't know we are going to Santorini, I think it will be OK," answered Hehu.

"Does everyone agree?" asked Pachai.

Everyone nodded. Hehu went back to the front desk and talked to Dimitris. Then everyone went upstairs.

6. TO SANTORINI

When Dimitris finished work at 4:00pm, he hurried back to his apartment to pack. He went to the airport from his apartment. Dimitris did not believe that Chrysa was in danger. But he was happy to be an interpreter and to have a weekend trip. He was very excited.

It will be good to earn some extra money. This is a good chance for me, he thought. *I will travel with these young people. They are so interesting! I will meet the daughter of Mr Melias! This could be good for my future. The Melias family will be happy to know their daughter is safe. They will be pleased with me.*

The others met in the coffee shop at 4:30pm. Pachai went to talk to Vasilis on the front desk.

"We have been invited to have dinner with friends in Corinth," he said. "We plan to stay the night and go sightseeing tomorrow. Please keep our suites for us. We will be back."

Dimitris got to the airport early. He waited by the check-in counter. He felt a little nervous. Then he saw the five friends arrive. They were all carrying small bags. They wore jeans and T-shirts. They looked strong and confident.

They look like an A-team or something, he thought. *I know that everything is OK. Mrs Melias is a little crazy. She worries too much. But if something is wrong, these people will know what to do.*

The flight to Santorini was wonderful. They all looked out of the windows at the brilliant blue sea. Then they could see the island. As the plane got closer to the airport, they could see the shining white buildings.

"It's a magical place," said Shelley. "I wish we were coming for a vacation, and not a rescue!"

Jarmo was sitting next to Shelley. "We don't know it's a rescue," he said. "This might all be a crazy mistake!"

Shelley turned to Jarmo. Jarmo was shocked to see that Shelley was crying.

"It's not a mistake," she said. "I have a very bad feeling. I am very frightened for Chrysa. I think something is very wrong."

Jarmo hugged Shelley.

"It will be OK," he said. "Remember St Brieuc and Tokyo and Sydney? Things were bad there too. But we are always OK. We will find Chrysa and make sure she is safe."

Shelley dried her eyes. "I hope so."

At the airport, Dimitris helped Pachai hire a rental car. They walked out to the parking lot to drive the car away. It was a large car suitable for six people. Pachai opened the driver's door and looked in.

"Good," he said. "It has GPS. Dimitris, would you please programme this address into the GPS? He handed Dimitris Mrs Melias' notes. Pachai got into the driver's seat. Hehu sat beside him. Dimitris climbed into the back seats of the car together with Jarmo, Akina and Shelley.

Pachai drove out of the airport and followed the signs for Akrotiri. Dimitris was surprised.

"Where are you going?" he asked. "There are many good hotels near the airport."

"We're going directly to the great-grandmother's house," answered Pachai. "We can worry about our hotel later."

I thought we would go to a nice hotel, thought Dimitris. *I thought we would have a wonderful meal with wine, and a good sleep. Then tomorrow, after breakfast we would visit the great-grandmother. I don't like this!*

"But we can't visit such an old woman so late at night!" he said. "It is not polite."

"Maybe we won't knock on the door," said Hehu. "But we want to look. If everything seems OK, we can go back tomorrow."

After driving for 30 minutes, Pachai stopped the car.

"The map shows we have to take a small road from here. It seems the house we want is at the end of the road. It is the only house near there. But I can't see the road."

Hehu climbed out of the car and walked around. He came back and said, "I can't see a real road. But I can see a narrow path like a walking track. Maybe that is the way to the house."

Pachai drove very carefully and slowly down the narrow path. After about 500m, they saw the house.

"Oh," said Akina. "It is so beautiful."

The house stood alone on top of a steep cliff. It was white with a blue roof. Below the house was the sea. It was shining in the setting sun. A small van was parked next to the house.

Pachai drove up and stopped the car next to the van. They all looked up at the house.

"I think the entrance is there," said Dimitris pointing to some steps. At the top of the steps was a heavy wooden door. The door was open.

"OK," said Pachai. "Someone is home. Shall we go to the door and ask for Chrysa?"

Everyone got out of the car and walked up the steps.

"Please call out, Dimitris," said Pachai. "We don't want to frighten the old lady."

Dimitris went close to the open door. "Hello!" he called out in Greek. "Hello! May we speak to you please? We are friends of the Melias family!"

There was no answer. Hehu was standing next to Dimitris. He looked through the door. He listened. "I'm going into the house," he said.

"No! No!" shouted Dimitris. "You can't do that!"

"Yes I can," answered Hehu. "Everyone wait here."

He disappeared through the open door. Very soon he came back.

"Pachai," he said. "I need you. Everyone else stay here. Don't come in."

Pachai went up to the door and followed Hehu inside the house.

7. THE HOUSE OF HORROR

Pachai walked into a square hallway. There was a steep staircase in front of him, but Hehu said, "This way." He pointed down a hallway to the left. Pachai followed Hehu into a large room. The walls and floors were stone. The windows looked out over the ocean. In the middle of the room, a very old woman was lying on her back. She was covered with a blanket. Her eyes were closed. Her hands were folded over her chest above the blanket. Someone had put flowers in her hands.

Pachai hurried to look at her. He knelt on the floor, and touched her face and hands.

"The great-grandmother?" he said softly. "She's been dead for a while – maybe more than a day." He stood up and looked around the room. He pointed to a large wooden chair near a window. "I guess she died in that chair. Someone moved her."

"Now come and see this," said Hehu. "Come into the next room."

It was the kitchen. There was a black iron stove against one wall. Pachai looked at the big wooden table in the middle of the room. He saw a chopping board and a knife, and a pile of vegetables.

"Here," said Hehu. He walked to the other side of the table. Through an open door, Pachai could see a small garden. But on the floor, next to the door was another woman. She was wearing a black dress and a white apron.

"I think maybe she was the housekeeper," said Hehu. "She's dead too, isn't she?"

Pachai looked at the blood on the floor. He knelt down next to the woman and put his hand on her neck. "Yes, she's dead too." He turned the body over. He pointed to the blood that covered the front of the white apron. "She was killed with a knife, I think."

He got up from the kitchen floor and walked back through the house to the main door. He stood at the top of the steps and called out. "Dimitris! Please call the police. Tell them there has been a murder. They must come quickly."

He turned to go back inside. "Stop!" shouted Shelley. "What are you doing?"

"Hehu and I must search the rest of the house." He disappeared.

Shelley and Akina held each other. "Is it Chrysa? Is she dead?" asked Akina.

Dimitris was talking on his smartphone. Jarmo was looking towards the sea.

"Listen," he said. "Can you hear that?"

Shelley and Akina listened hard.

"I can't hear anything," said Shelley. "Oh, yes I can. It's very soft. Is it singing?"

Dimitris put his phone in his pocket. "The police are coming," he said. "They will be here in about twenty minutes."

Jarmo walked slowly and carefully down the side of the house towards the sea. Akina and Shelley followed him.

Dimitris didn't want to go with them. But then he thought, *If I don't go with them, I will be alone. I don't like this. I am very frightened.*

He hurried after the two young women.

At the end of the house was a wide terrace. Many metres below the terrace, was the sea. Jarmo hurried towards the terrace, then stopped suddenly.

"Oh, no!" he whispered.

Akina and Shelley were standing close behind him. The three looked at a young man sitting on a low wall at the edge of terrace. Dimitris waited at the corner of the house. He could see everything, and he was too frightened to go closer.

"It must be Michalis," said Akina very quietly.

Michalis looked terrible. There was blood on his shirt. His face was dirty. They could see he had been crying. He was holding Chrysa in his arms. Her eyes were closed. Her head was hanging down. He was rocking her like a baby. He was singing to her.

"Is she dead?" asked Akina.

Shelley stared. "No. I don't think so. I think I can see her breathing."

Jarmo called out. "Michalis! We have come to help you. I will come and take Chrysa. I think she needs a doctor."

Michalis looked up. "Who are you?"

"We are Chrysa's friends," answered Jarmo.

"Oh, yes! Chrysa's friends. You took her away from me! Before she met you, she liked me. I knew she would marry me. You can't have her! She's mine!"

"Why did you bring Chrysa here?" asked Jarmo. "Her mother is very worried. We came to find her."

"I hoped Chrysa would love me. When my father died, Mr Melias promised I could have Chrysa. I waited. One day, Chrysa would marry me. I knew it.

"I was the boss of my father's company. I tried to make the business more successful. I wanted to be richer than Georgios Melias. But I made some bad choices. I lost money. So I started to gamble. I wanted to save my father's company. But I lost more and more money. Soon there was no money left. Then I thought, 'If I marry Chrysa, her father will give me money. He will not want his daughter to be poor.' I made a plan. I would bring Chrysa here. She would love my great-grandmother. Everyone loved my great-grandmother. Then my great-grandmother would tell Chrysa to marry me. It would be OK. But everything went wrong."

"What happened?" asked Jarmo. He was trying to get closer and closer to Michalis.

Dimitris was still hiding by the corner of the house. Shelley and Akina were looking at Jarmo, Michalis and Chrysa. They weren't looking at anything else. But Dimitris could see Pachai and Hehu. They were at the other end of the terrace.

"Don't come any closer!" Michalis saw that Jarmo was near to him. "Move back or I'll kill her!"

"OK. OK. Sorry." Jarmo took a few steps back. Jarmo saw Michalis had one arm around Chrysa's shoulders. There was a knife in his hand.

"What happened?" asked Jarmo again.

"She wouldn't come with me. She wouldn't come to visit my great-grandmother. I was angry. It was a good plan! But Chrysa wouldn't do what I wanted.

"I got drugs. I went to the Melias house. I went in. I went upstairs. Chrysa was in her room. The door was open. I watched her. She was using her computer. She was so happy! It made me crazy. I hid in the room next door. She went downstairs, and I went into her bedroom. She had a glass of fruit juice next to her computer. I put the drugs in the fruit juice. I went back to the room next door and waited. Chrysa came upstairs. I waited a long time. When I heard no noise, I went to her bedroom. She was lying on the bed. After that it was easy."

"What was easy?" asked Jarmo.

Michalis didn't answer. He looked down at Chrysa in his arms. He started singing again.

Shelley put her hand on Jarmo's back. She said something. Jarmo looked to his right. He saw Pachai and Hehu. They were moving slowly towards Michalis.

Shelley, Akina and Jarmo couldn't move. They knew that Michalis might do something crazy. They knew they must not look at Pachai and Hehu. They knew that Michalis must not see the other men.

"Michalis!" said Jarmo loudly. "Look at me! You must tell me! What happened?"

8. NOTHING LEFT

Dimitris watched the scene. Michalis could not see him, but Dimitris could see Pachai and Hehu. Suddenly Hehu disappeared.

Where has he gone? thought Dimitris. Then he saw a large hand on the top of the low wall. Hehu had climbed over the wall. He was pulling himself along the top of the cliff. He was getting closer and closer to Michalis and Chrysa.

"What happened?" said Jarmo again. "Look at me, Michalis."

"I brought Chrysa here on my yacht. She was unconscious. Every time she started to wake up, I drugged her again. I stole a van, and I brought her here to my great-grandmother's house. I told my great-grandmother everything. She was so angry with me! She shouted at me! Then she died! One moment she was shouting at me, and the next moment she was dead. I killed her!" screamed Michalis.

"It's OK," said Jarmo. "She was very old and sick. I'm sure you didn't kill her."

"I did," answered Michalis. "Then I killed the housekeeper too. I killed her with this knife."

He waved the knife at Jarmo. Then he put it back against Chrysa's throat.

"There is nothing left. No money. No Chrysa. She doesn't want me. But no one else will have her."

He stood up. He had his arm around Chrysa's neck. She was hanging like a doll.

"He's going to jump!" shouted Dimitris and closed his eyes. He heard loud noises and shouting. Then there was silence. He opened his eyes. Akina was standing next to him. "Call an ambulance for Chrysa," she said. Then she was gone.

Dimitris was shaking. He took out his smartphone and made the call. Then he looked across the terrace. Chrysa was lying on the ground. Shelley and Pachai were kneeling next to her. He couldn't see Michalis. Jarmo and Hehu were standing next to the wall looking down.

"Where's Michalis?" asked Dimitris.

"Down there," said Jarmo, pointing to the sea. Dimitris looked down. Far below, he could see Michalis. He had fallen on some rocks at the edge of the water.

"Can Chrysa drink anything?" It was Akina. She was walking along the terrace with a glass of water.

"I will try to give her a little," said Pachai. "Thank you. She has been drugged for days. I hope the ambulance comes soon."

Dimitris looked at his phone. It was only 25 minutes since he called the police. Everything happened so quickly, he thought. It seems like I made that call hours ago.

Just then, the police arrived. Ten minutes later, the ambulance came.

Some of the police spoke English, but Dimitris was busy interpreting and explaining.

Jarmo, Pachai, Shelley, Hehu and Akina sat on the terrace and waited. The paramedics put Chrysa into the ambulance. Shelley and Akina wanted to go with her, but the police said, 'no'. The police said they would contact Chrysa's family.

"You must stay here," said the police. "The situation is very bad. You must answer many questions. Later we will take you to the main police station in Fira."

The police asked one of the ambulance staff to look at Hehu. His hands and face were covered in cuts and bruises.

"What happened?" asked the ambulance woman. Hehu explained, and Dimitris interpreted. "I was on the other side of the wall. When Michalis jumped, I tried to catch him. It was difficult. I held him with one hand for a short time, but I could not hang on. He was fighting me. He fell. But it was enough time for Pachai and Jarmo to take hold of Chrysa and pull her back over the wall."

It was almost midnight when the police drove them all back to the police station in the main town. Hehu and Pachai travelled in a police car with Dimitris. Jarmo, Akina and Shelley went in the rental car with a police driver.

At the police station, they sat in an interview room with a guard. A young policeman brought them coffee.

"Wonderful!" smiled Jarmo. "Do you realise we haven't had anything to eat or drink since four thirty pm?"

"Do you know anything about Chrysa?" Akina asked the young policeman.

"My English is not very good," he answered. "Her parents came. They came in a private plane. Maybe she is OK."

"Do you know anything else?" Dimitris asked him in Greek.

"They are checking the story. They must find out if it is true," said the young policeman.

"Of course it is true!" Dimitris was angry, but he was also frightened.

"Maybe. But three people are dead. Maybe the old lady's death was natural, but the others were not. Everything must be checked."

He went away.

"You know," said Akina. "It was so sad when Michalis said there was nothing left. I am pleased Chrysa will be OK. But now I am very tired."

She took her shoes off, lay down on the floor and went to sleep. Shelley put her head on the table and slept too.

Jarmo, Pachai and Hehu drank their coffee and chatted quietly.

They are a little strange, thought Dimitris. *They are in a police station in a foreign country. It is one am in the morning. They don't speak the language. But they are very calm. They don't seem worried at all.*

Two hours later, a policeman came to the room. Then an older policeman came in.

"You can go now. We have checked your stories. It seems they are true. There are two cars waiting to take you to a hotel."

"How is Chrysa?" asked Pachai.

"Her parents are with her. The doctors say she will be fine."

"Oh, good," said Shelley sleepily. "Just take me to a bed. This table is very uncomfortable to sleep on.".

9. IT'S ONLY THURSDAY

Shelley woke up. She looked around the room. It was very big. The bed was wide and soft. The sun was shining.

Oh, I need a shower. When we arrived here, I fell onto this bed and I didn't even clean my teeth! What time is it?

She looked at her smartphone. "It's noon," she said out loud. *I have slept for nine hours! What day is it? Thursday! It's only Thursday! I don't believe it.*

She went to the bathroom. She spent a long time in the shower. She washed her hair and found clean clothes.

Now I feel better. But I'm so hungry. She looked at the hotel information booklet. She saw a picture of a terrace restaurant. It had a buffet. *That looks nice!*

She called Akina's smartphone, but Akina did not answer.

Still sleeping, thought Shelley. She sent a text.

--- *Gone to terrace restaurant to eat.* ---

She sent the same text to Hehu. An answer came back quickly

--- *We're there already. Hurry before we eat all the food.* ---

Shelley laughed and hurried to the elevator.

Shelley loaded her tray with food and joined the men at their table. They ate in silence. Everyone was very hungry, and everyone was still thinking about what had happened.

Finally, Pachai, Hehu and Shelley had eaten enough. But not Jarmo.

"I need some more," he said.

"You are amazing," said Pachai. "You eat three times as much as me. You eat much more than Hehu, and he is twice your size."

Jarmo laughed. "I want to be as big as him when I grow up!"

He took his tray and went towards the buffet tables.

When he came back, Akina was with him. She had a small plate of food and a fruit juice.

"We have to hurry," she said. "The front desk called my room. Mr and Mrs Melias will be here in fifteen minutes. They want to talk to us."

"This is a very expensive hotel," said Pachai. "The one in Athens is five star but this is super-luxury. I am sure the police are not paying for this."

"No," answered Hehu. "I guess Mr Melias is paying. So I am sure he is not angry with us."

"I hope he is very sorry!" said Shelley. "He should have listened to his wife. Chrysa almost died. Where's Dimitris? That's terrible! I forgot about Dimitris! Is he still sleeping?"

"It's OK, Shelley," said Hehu. "He wasn't in his room so I asked the front desk. The police came to get him. He has to sign his statement. He'll be back soon."

"I have something to ask you," said Akina. "It's about the money from Mrs Melias. This is my plan."

They listened to Akina's plan and everyone agreed it was the best idea.

"There's Mr and Mrs Melias," said Jarmo. "Over by the restaurant doors. Dimitris is with them."

Mr Melias was talking to the headwaiter. In seconds, four waiters came to their table. They picked up Akina's and Jarmo's food and the coffee cups and glasses.

"Please follow us," said one of the waiters.

They walked after the waiters and into the hotel. The waiters took them to a private room.

Mr Melias ran towards them. He hugged Akina and Shelley. He kissed them. Then he hugged Pachai, Hehu and Jarmo. He was crying.

"Thank you!" he shouted. "The police told me everything. You are not Greek! You are young. But you are heroes. You saved my daughter!"

"It's OK, Mr Melias," said Pachai. "It wasn't anything special."

"No," said Hehu. "We were lucky. We were there at the right time."

Mr Melias calmed down. Suddenly he looked very old. He sat down. He waved at the other chairs. Everyone sat down.

"That's not true. It is nice of you to say it was nothing, but you saved my daughter. It was my fault. I didn't listen to my wife."

"Will Chrysa be OK?" asked Akina.

"Yes. The doctors say she will recover soon. She is young and strong. We will take her to Athens today. She will have the best hospital and the best doctors. I want you to stay here."

"But we want to see Chrysa," said Shelley.

"Not now. She must rest and be quiet. Tomorrow my private plane will come back here. My pilot will fly you to Athens. You can go back to my hotel. On Saturday, you can see Chrysa."

"OK," said Pachai.

Just then Mr Melias' phone rang. "Excuse me," he said and walked out of the room to talk the phone call.

Akina and Shelley turned to Mrs Melias.

"Is everything OK?" asked Akina.

Mrs Melias looked very tired, but she also looked happy. "Yes. It is all right now. I thank you. I couldn't do anything, so I decided to trust Chrysa's friends. It was the best thing. Now Chrysa is safe."

"Please don't judge Michalis too much," said Jarmo. "His mind was not normal."

"I understand," said Mrs Melias. "Poor Michalis. He kidnapped Chrysa, and killed the housekeeper. Maybe it is better he died."

"Just one thing," said Akina. "The money. You gave Shelley and me a lot of money. We can't keep it. I took out a little of your money to pay Dimitris, but the rest of it is here. She took two envelopes out of her bag. She gave a small envelope to Dimitris, and a much bigger one to Mrs Melias.

Mrs Melias pushed it back at Akina.

"No!" she said. "It's yours."

"No," said Hehu. "We don't take money to help our friends."

"We want to give it to the family of the housekeeper," said Shelley. "Could you arrange that, Mrs Melias?"

"I can do that," said Mrs Melias. She picked up the envelope and put it in her bag. "You are unusual young people. It seems you don't care about money."

"We care about each other," said Pachai quietly. "We care about our friends. Money is not so important."

Mr Melias came back into the room. "We have to go," he said. "Come, Sofia. You come too, Dimitris. We will take you back to Athens. You did well. I must think about your future."

Dimitris looked very happy. He followed Mr and Mrs Melias out of the room.

10. A HOLIDAY IN GREECE

Later in the day, the police asked them to go down to the police station. Their statements were all printed out in English, and they read and signed them. They swam in the hotel pool, and then went for a walk.

Santorini was a most beautiful and interesting place. They loved it.

"We'll come back one day with Chrysa," said Akina. "It is not the same without her."

"I wonder if she will ever want to come here again," said Jarmo. "She had a very bad experience."

On Friday, they went back to Athens. They went sightseeing and shopping. Everyone was quiet, and a little depressed. There was no news from Chrysa. She didn't call them. Everyone was worried.

On Saturday a limousine came and drove them to Chrysa's home. Chrysa was in bed. She was very pale and tired, but she was pleased to see them.

"I remember making plans for our vacation," she said. "But then I don't remember anything. I hate it. The police told me what happened. Michalis is dead. I was there. I can't believe it. I can't believe I don't remember!"

Chrysa was very upset.

"We won't talk about it, Chrysa," said Hehu gently. "It happened. It's finished. It is in the past. We will talk about other things. How is your Spanish study? I am sure I know more than you do!"

"No way!" smiled Chrysa. "I have been studying very hard."

They went to see Chrysa every morning. In the afternoons they went sightseeing, shopping and walking. They went to small bars with music in the evenings. They enjoyed themselves very much.

Then the next Tuesday, it was time to leave. Everyone had flights out of Athens in the late evening. The limousine came to get them as usual. Chrysa was waiting on the terrace for them. She was much better. She looked a lot more cheerful.

"You came to Greece to see me. I wanted to show you my country. But I was a very bad tour guide," she said. "I will do better next time!"

They chatted and drank coffee. They talked about where they would like to go next. Then it was time to go. Chrysa had an appointment with her doctors.

They kissed and hugged. "See you soon!"

"Until next time!"

Mrs Melias walked down to the limousine with them.

"Chrysa is well in her body," she said. "But her mind is still troubled. She can't remember, and she worries. You are very good for her. When you plan your next vacation, please invite her."

"Invite her?" said Jarmo. "If Chrysa cannot come, there will be no vacation. We are a team."

Mrs Melias smiled. "You are good friends to my daughter."

She took a bag from her arm. "You would not take any money from me. But you must take these gifts. I hope they will remind you that Greece is a wonderful country."

She gave each of them a box wrapped in silver paper.

She hugged all of them before they climbed into the limousine. She waved as they drove away.

From the terrace, Chrysa waved too. *I will be better soon. The next vacation will be somewhere wonderful.*

THANK YOU

Thank you for reading Different Seas. (Word count: 21,305) We hope you enjoyed it.

If you would like to read more graded readers, please visit our website http://www.italkyoutalk.com

Other Level 3 graded readers include
A Dangerous Weekend
A Holiday to Remember
Akiko and Amy Part 1
Akiko and Amy Part 2
Akiko and Amy Part 3
Be My Valentine
Enjoy Your Business Trip
Enjoy Your Homestay
I Need a Friend
Old Jack's Ghost Stories from England (1)
Old Jack's Ghost Stories from England (2)
Old Jack's Ghost Stories from Ireland
Old Jack's Ghost Stories from Japan
Old Jack's Ghost Stories from Scotland
Old Jack's Ghost Stories from Wales
Party Time!

Different Seas

Stories for Christmas
The Curse
Together Again
Who is Holly?

ABOUT THE AUTHOR

I Talk You Talk Press is a Japan-based publisher of language textbooks, graded readers and language learning/teaching resources.

Our team is made up of highly experienced language teachers and translators, who have all studied at least one additional language to an advanced level.

This experience enables us to design our materials from the perspective of both the teacher and the learner. We consult with both teachers and language learners when designing our textbooks and graded readers, and test our materials extensively in the classroom before publication.

We are a fast-growing press, and currently publish graded readers for learners of English. We publish new graded readers monthly.

www.ingramcontent.com/pod-product-compliance
Lightning Source LLC
Chambersburg PA
CBHW032211040426
42449CB00005B/534